Dr. Tesfaye Biftu
An Exemplar of Expertise
in DRUG DISCOVERY

Copyright © 2024 Publisher Beniam T. Biftu and Moa T. Biftu

ISBN 9781947841864

All rights reserved. No part of this book may be reproduced or transmitted in any form or by any means without written permission from the publisher.

Table of Content

Overview	v
Part I: BIOGRAPHY	1
Chapter 1: Where It All Started	3
Chapter 2: The Years of Growth	11
Chapter 3: The Exposure to First Foreign Education	20
Chapter 4: The Trip to France - Higher Education In Normandy	26
Chapter 5: Higher Studies in the United States of America	33
Chapter 6: Post Graduate Studies at Brandeis University	40
Chapter 7: Tesfaye's Return to Ethiopia Amid Political Unrest	45
Chapter 8: How Does It Feel to Be a Globally Recognized Medicinal Chemist?	64
Chapter 9: The Settlement of an Ethiopian American Family in the United States	75
Chapter 10: Retirement Life	81
Chapter 11: Community and Business Engagement	84
Chapter 12: International Recognition, Honors, and Achievements	90
Part II: VIEWS AND OPINIONS	95
Chapter 13: Observations on the Political and Historical Systems of Ethiopia	96
Chapter 14: Opinions on Religion, Ethnic Politics, and Ethnicity in Ethiopia	108

Chapter 15: Views on The US Political System	114
Chapter 16: Perspective on Humanity's Future Potential	123
Part III: DRUG DISCOVERIES, PUBLICATIONS AND PATENTS	125
Chapter 17: Important Drug Discoveries by Dr. Tesfaye Biftu	126
Chapter 18: Dr. Tesfaye's Major Publications and Patents	157
Annex I: Sample Scientific Publications	160
ANNEX II: Sample International Lectures by Tesfaye Biftu	169
ANNEX III: USA Patents	171

Overview

Dr. Tesfaye Biftu is a remarkable Ethiopian-American scientist of international renown. He was born and raised in the little town of Agaro in southwest Ethiopia and completed his PhD at Brandeis University and his MBA in management from Rutgers University in the US.

Following a brief academic career, he first worked as a medicinal chemist for Merck & Co. before moving on to CytoMed Inc. as a Senior Director of Medicinal Chemistry. He eventually returned to Merck, where he successively worked as a Distinguished Senior Investigator and the Director of Discovery Chemistry.

Dr. Biftu is the author and co-author of more than 70 manuscripts and book chapters as well as around 100 US and foreign patents. His work has focused on developing drugs for treating inflammatory, cardiovascular, metabolic, and infectious diseases as well as obesity, thrombosis, inflammation, and other human and animal health issues.

He was the project leader and a prominent contributor to the discovery of various therapeutic products, including Marizev™, the Once-Weekly DPP-4 Inhibitor anti-diabetic agent and Januvia™

Dr. Tesfaye is one of only a few scientists who has received over 100 international and US patents for his contribution to pharmaceutical sciences, some solo, and others in contribution with others. It's nothing short of a miracle, given that he began school in Ethiopia, where modern education was only emerging at the time, and that he completed his schooling there.

And how did he manage to achieve so much as a man of color in a world-famous pharmaceutical corporation in the United States?

Tesfaye Biftu was able to present a fine scientific article initially when he was in Grade 9. He dedicates his success to his father's great support, his mother's love, kindness, and care, his beloved teacher Ato Tesfaye Admassu's proven teaching techniques and his wife Tersit Tadesse's relentless support during his stay in the United States.

Those who come from modest backgrounds will undoubtedly be inspired by reading the astounding tales of this genius and come to understand that everything is possible for someone with the drive to pursue their goals.

This respected medicinal chemist is more than simply a brilliant individual who spends all his time alone in an experimental laboratory. He has a good heart and is a modest person.

He had a very close bond with his father, Biftu Diko, also known as Aba Fira Biftu, who receives most of the praise for his son's accomplishments.

Dr. Tesfaye Biftu, for his part, had previously risked his life to free his father from the Derg, one of history's most violent dictatorships, from jail in Ethiopia.

His bravery and dedication are admirable. His wife, children, and the Ethiopian community in the United States have naturally benefited from his commitment to showing people love and care. In both the USA and Ethiopia, he has been able to find time to contribute to the causes important to his community.

Dr. Tesfaye comprehends what it takes to be an Ethiopian makes him the ideal role model for millions of Ethiopians.

In addition, he and his beloved wife, Tersit Taddasse Biftu, are both of mixed ethnic heritage, and Dr. Tesfaye eloquently argues that no Ethiopian can claim to be fully from this or that ethnic group because no one knows for certain which other groups were associated with one another in previous generations.

Anyone with a human interest will find the accounts of Dr. Tesfaye's drug discovery and medicinal research quite fascinating. And particularly, the young talent from underprivileged backgrounds with bigger goals and potential have much to learn from Dr. Tesfaye.

This is especially true for young readers of African descent, mainly Ethiopians, who can naturally relate to Dr. Tesfaye.

He is not just a great scientist but an influencer and role model in whom Ethiopians take great pride.

Part I: BIOGRAPHY

Chapter 1: Where It All Started

Tesfaye Biftu, the renowned medicinal chemist, was born and raised in Agaro. The small hamlet of Agaro served as the starting point for everything in his life.

Ethiopian coffee producers primarily inhabit the town of Agaro, which is also the source of Arabica coffee. Due to the work opportunities it provides, it draws individuals from many regions of Ethiopia.

In the 1950-60s, Agaro was the center of the Ethiopian economy. It is where the Arabica coffee variety, popularly known as the "Green Gold," was produced and is the country's largest producer of it.

Since meeting by fate, Ato Biftu Diko, also known as Aba Fira Biftu, and Wo. Truenesh Alemu have lived happily ever after in Agaro. By working hard, they were able to amass enough wealth.

Due to their kindness and modesty, they also won the respect of their town.

Despite having many wonderful things in their lives, the tragic loss of their infants left them with deeply broken hearts.

Two offspring, a boy and a girl, were born. Sadly, for reasons they were unaware of, their infant children died. The parents were really anxious about this.

A few months after the passing of her last child, W.o Truenesh Alemu became pregnant again, even though she had not yet fully recovered from the trauma caused by the untimely deaths of her two kids.

W.o Truenesh and her devoted spouse had conflicting emotions about the pregnancy. They were happy because they desperately wanted a child. In this way, the announcement of the unborn child gave their lives a glimmer of hope. However, they were also terrified that the newborn may contract the unknown illness that killed their other children.

As a result, they started searching diligently for a solution to protect their children from the dreadful sickness that had already led to the deaths of their two children.

They sought advice from friends, family members, and people of both Christian and Muslim faiths who they believed could offer suggestions on how to ensure the healthy birth of their unborn baby.

The Muslim friends proposed traveling to Dembi, a little town a few kilometers outside of Agaro on the road to Gore, Illubabor, and asking the well-known cleric Sheik Dembi to lead a prayer. They did as told.

The Sheik advised them to give the boy they were expecting the name Kedir. They also prayed to the saints, pleading for their mercy as devoted Orthodox Christians.

And soon enough, Ato Biftu Diko and Wo. Truenesh Alemu welcomed a baby boy.

The newborn kid was given the name Tesfaye by his mother right away, and he was baptized as Sahle Michael in St. Michael's church.

The new baby was given the nickname Kediro, short for Kedir, by the Muslim majority of Agaro's inhabitants.

Tesfaye, which means "my hope" in Amharic, was a nod to the parent's hope that the infant would survive the terrible, fatal illness.

Ato Biftu's family had guests from the neighborhood on the day the child was born to celebrate the baby's healthy delivery.

Fortunately, Ato Biftu and W.o. Truenesh's newborn child escaped the mysterious fatal condition, became healthy, and flourished. His parents were sure their prayers had been heard. In return, they strictly upheld the religious vows they had made.

Ato Biftu Diko: The Role Model and Father of Tesfaye Biftu

Ato Biftu Diko   Wo. Trunesh Alemu

Ato Biftu was born in the ancient Illu Abbabor province in a distinctive region named Didu Tulama. He was better known by his people as Aba Fira, which means generous. He is an Oromo, one of Ethiopia's most populous ethnic groups. Eleven of his siblings still resided in Illubabor while he relocated to Agaro in pursuit of a better life for himself.

His aspiration as a youngster was to succeed greatly in business. When he was just fourteen years old, he began working in business, primarily by traveling with traders. These traders were involved in the trade of coffee from Illu Abbabor to the former Kaffa region.

As a young dreamer, he experienced many difficulties in realizing his dream of becoming a successful trader. He received one Maria Theresa Thaler, a silver bullion coin that served as money in the early era of Emperor Haile Selassie, every month. In pursuit of his success, Ato Biftu used to tour for weeks across ranges of several hundred kilometers with the merchants. He continued this pattern by traveling to Addis Ababa and other locations for work, which gave him plenty of chances to explore other business alternatives.

After considering various business opportunities, Ato Biftu ultimately decided to relocate permanently to Agaro, where he was convinced that coffee dealing was a safer, more lucrative endeavor.

He enjoyed his work, which helped him succeed as a businessman. He didn't have a formal education, but he was good with numbers because of his persistent personal effort.

Aside from that, he wanted his son Tesfaye (Kediro) to flourish academically and accomplish what he himself had missed out on as a child. This attitude made Ato Biftu Diko different from other traders who wanted their kids to follow in their footsteps. To ensure this, he sent his beloved son and the kids of his family to public schools.

Tesfaye remembers a time when his father's house was home to 18 kids living there, and his father was paying for their meals, accommodation and school expenses. The majority of them later achieved academic success. Some even held PhDs, including Dr. Tesfaye Bekele.

Tesfaye states the following about his parents' contribution to his success:

"My parents had a significant impact on my successes.

My father put in a lot of effort. I don't recall ever having breakfast with my dad when I was a kid. Except for Sundays, he was always at work from 5 a.m. until 7 p.m. every day. I used to go on trips with him in the summer, when schools were out, to various provinces of Ethiopia including Gonder, Eritrea, Wollo and Sidamo. Also, we visited nearby countries like Kenya and Uganda. My father was a devout man. He valued hard work and approached life with optimism. He advised me to work hard in my studies, do well in school, and respect my teachers.

Despite having a demanding work schedule, he never skipped my school's family days. He was always there for me, encouraging and supporting me. Like most Ethiopians of his generation, he never chose companions based on their race, religion, or ethnicity."

Furthermore, Tesfaye mentioned that his beloved father taught him the value of helping those in need and being genuine and modest, among others. Ato Biftu Diko was universally acknowledged in his town for his generosity and compassion toward his entire family and strangers.

He took pleasure in helping those in need and was well renowned for giving others the chance to live better lives. Because of his kindness and compassion for others, his community gave him the name Aba Fira.

Tesfaye's parents tragically split up when he was four years old. Wo. Truenesh, Tesfaye's mother, received some of the family's riches. Also, Ato Biftu Diko had excellently constructed a home for her in Agaro town.

Their relationships remained cordial, pleasant, and accessible despite the split.

He lived with his father from Monday through Thursday once he started school. On Fridays, he would frequently see his mother and spend the weekend at home before returning to school on Monday. He felt entirely at ease there, and their separation never caused him discomfort.

"They were both approachable and helpful to me. To be honest, I didn't comprehend they had split up until I was old enough," Tesfaye recalls.

Following his divorce, Aba Fira married Wo. Abebech, a woman from Menz in the Northern Shoa region, and stayed in Agaro. She was well-known for her traditional family beliefs. In line with this, she fostered Tesfaye.

He remembers: *"I never realized she was my stepmother when I was a kid. She was incredibly compassionate and loving to me."*

Later in his life, Ato Biftu was blessed with more children: Yeshi, Seifu, Tsehai, Zewdu, Mebrat, Abinet and Kassech Biftu.

Tesfaye's Childhood Interests and Inclinations

Tesfaye valued academic study above participating in extracurricular activities compared to other kids of his age.

His family and teachers characterize his early demeanor as focused, peaceful, hardworking, and imaginative. Except for athletics, where his performance was less than stellar, he was intelligent in every discipline. He was a top student, from first grade to eighth grade, at Ras Desta Damtew School. He enjoyed watching various sports, although he didn't participate in many of them when he was younger.

Ato Biftu Diko always motivated his son to achieve academic success. Furthermore, Ato Biftu Diko had developed a strong relationship with his son and regularly monitored his progress throughout the years.

Additionally, he frequently purchased books on his travels to other places and had his son read them to him. Tesfaye passionately narrated the tales to his father. Such reading routines honed his reading abilities at a young age.

Ato Biftu Diko was self-taught and skilled in arithmetic. To the amazement of his acquaintances who went to formal education, he taught himself how to do mathematical computations.

He would say, *"Yesterday I purchased 120 quintals of coffee and delivered it to my business,"* and then urged his son to do the calculations. *"A quintal of coffee was 1200 birr in price. Would you calculate the 120 quintals' total cost for me?"*

Tesfaye often performed these computations with accuracy. He rarely gave incorrect responses. His father's motivating teachings enabled him to concentrate and pay attention.

Tesfaye also spent his summer breaks working hard, thanks to the encouragement of his father. During his summers in Addis Ababa, he learned a variety of skills. When he was only in Grade 4, he learned to type in Addis Ababa over the summer break.

He brought a typing machine back so he could practice more. He could type 60 words per minute even though he was only in Grade 5. His time spent on vacation in Addis Ababa also benefited his adjustment to city life, which eased his future academic endeavors. Tesfaye earned the first rank in each grade from first to eighth at Ras Desta Damtew School. His peers have great admiration for his accomplishments and outstanding skills in science and arts.

His peers, especially those who were his competitors, greatly appreciated his accomplishments and amazing skill.

In Grade 6, Tesfaye built up a small laboratory area after being impressed by his science teacher. He set it up with various laboratory supplies and reference materials, and he would conduct several scientific experiments at home. Once, with his friend Abraham Sere Berhan, he attempted to distill oil out of mud and charcoal. This was one of his earlier experiments at an early age.

Chapter 2: The Years of Growth

Tesfaye enrolled in Ras Desta Primary School in 1955, just a few years after Ethiopia's first formal curriculum was made public. The school bears the name of an anti-fascist revolutionary leader who was also the son-in-law of Emperor Haile Selassie.

When Tesfaye attended school, Ras Desta Primary School was the only educational facility in Agaro town. He started first grade at the school when he was five. His early school years are, therefore, not well-remembered by him.

He did, however, grow up to be one of the most exceptional and active students because of the excellent teachers he had and the tremendous support of his father.

Tesfaye firmly believes that his teachers significantly contributed to his early accomplishment, which provided a solid foundation for his eventual outstanding academic achievements.

Teklu Anno, Tesfaye Admasu and Tesfaye Biftu (left to right)

"I will always be grateful to my fourth-grade science teacher, Ato Tesfaye Admasu, who inspired me when I was a young student.

"My early interest in chemistry would not have been productive if it had not been for the mentorship and encouragement of my teacher, Ato Tesfaye Admasu."

"He was a genuine teacher with exceptional talent and dedication. I recall him having simply a certificate from the Teachers Training Institute (TTI). His innovative scientific performances, both theoretical and practical, significantly impacted me. I loved watching and learning about plants and minerals as a kid." Tesfaye recounts.

Not just Tesfaye Biftu, who admired his science teacher, Ato Tesfaye Admasu felt the same for him.

He remembered him even after 50 years when he said:

"Even after fifty years, I can still recall the names of my two brightest students from Ras Desta Damtew. First, Tesfaye Biftu and the other Teklu Anno. In my 35 years working in education, they are the most energetic students I have ever encountered. Their interests and dedication to science were very strong. Tesfaye, in particular, was extremely close to me. I was surprised to see that at that age, he could do original, astounding scientific experiments. He would also regularly ask me to assist him in addressing newer scientific problems, which he used quite effectively to study on his own. I did everything I could to support Tesfaye Biftu in using his exceptional gift to advance the area of research."

Ato Workeneh Sefi, an English language teacher at Ras Desta Damtew Primary School in Agaro, was another inspiring teacher who significantly contributed to Tesfaye Biftu's achievement.

"Ato Workeneh Sefi, who several years later became the deputy governor of Shoa province, was one of the best educators who successfully gave his students exemplary English language abilities. He did not confine himself to the common topics covered in the textbooks. Instead, he provided regular assignments to encourage his students to develop their writing, reading, and listening abilities in the English language," Tesfaye explains.

The High School Years: General Wingate

Tesfaye Biftu could write the finest scientific papers at the Grade 9 level owing to his father's incredible support, his mother's undying love, warmth, and attention, and Ato Workeneh Sefi's credible teaching skills.

One of these scientific pieces that Tesfaye wrote at Bahir Dar Polytechnic Institute when he was in Grade 9 was published in the graduating class bulletin of 1963.

Reunion at Ras Desta Damtew Elementary School

One of the top secondary high schools in the country, General Wingate Senior Secondary School in Addis Ababa, was named after British Army commander Order Charles Wingate.

Only students who achieved the highest scores on the 8th-grade national examination and aced several additional tests were eligible to enroll in General Wingate Senior School.

Tesfaye and his two other classmates were the only ones chosen from Agaro's Ras Desta Damtew School to sit for the entrance exam. His two friends were Teklu Anno, a prominent textile engineer in the US, and Abraham Sereke Berhan, a Capitan in the Ethiopian Airlines.

As part of the evaluation process for admittance to the institution, all three had taken written tests over three consecutive days.

Tesfaye's transition to General Wingate Secondary School was significant in his academic career. All new students participated in a one-month orientation program. The goal was to group students based on how well they studied. Students were divided into three groups by the end of the month: 9A, 9B, and 9C.

Class 9A consisted of the top performers, Class 9B had students who performed decently, and Class 9C was grouped with students who needed assistance and supervision.

Out of the approximately 100 students that were enrolled in the school, Tesfaye recalls that only around 20 kids were eligible for 9A class.

The curriculum was created with the best secondary education standards in mind.

Because the kids came from all regions of the county, they had the chance to meet people from diverse economic and social backgrounds.

Student dormitories were divided into three groups according to color: Blue House, Green House, and Red House.

Similar to a military camp, education in the school was quite regimented. Classes typically ran from 8:30 in the morning to 5:00 in the afternoon. After dinner, the kids had a brief break, and most played basketball.

Tesfaye managed to play basketball quite brilliantly at Wingate despite minimal interest in athletics throughout his primary school years.

In the evening, the students returned to their classes to study until 10PM, under the rigorous supervision of the designated supervising professors.

Tesfaye would finish his schoolwork and other assignments in time to read more books. He used to read fiction novels from the school library.

Bahir Dar Polytechnic Institute- Sudden Change of Plans

Although he was doing well in his studies and had gotten excellent midterm scores while attending General Wingate Secondary School in Addis Ababa, Tesfaye heard about the newly opened Polytechnic Institute in Bahir Dar. It was during his first academic year. In addition, it was stated in the news that one of the Institute's four main academic specialties was industrial chemistry.

Tesfaye Biftu was quite intrigued because Chemistry was his major subject of interest. And that's when he immediately decided to drop out of General Wingate Secondary School.

Tesfaye chose to go and enroll in the Bahir Dar Polytechnic Institute after making sure that Industrial Chemistry was one of the areas of study. Despite not knowing if the Institute would accept him or not, he decided to give it his all and left right away for Bahir Dar, which is 550 kilometers from Addis Ababa.

He decided to keep it a secret from everyone. Even his father was not to be informed because he feared he might persuade him to reconsider his choice.

Since his father was aware that Wingate Secondary School was one of the few elite institutions in the country, he wouldn't have permitted his son to leave it for a new name in the market.

Even though he mainly chose to enroll in the new Institute on his own, he soon realized that he wanted money to get to Bahir Dar and apply for admission to the school.

As a result, he chose to borrow money from one of his father's best friends, Ato Abdul Zemed Nuru, an accomplished businessman from Agaro who happened to be in Addis Ababa at the time.

Tesfaye informed him of his intention to travel to Bahir Dar and register at the Institute.

As he was confident that Ato Biftu Diko would compensate him, Ato Abdul Zemed handed him the required money.

The following day, Tesfaye Biftu went to an Ethiopian Airlines ticket counter, purchased a 43 *Birr* ticket for his travel to Bahir Dar, and took off the next day.

Tesfaye slept in a motel for the first night in Bahir Dar, then left early in the morning to apply for admission to the polytechnic Institute. The complex is encircled by several trees and is located next to Lake Tana. It made him even more motivated to study at the Institute for his favorite subject.

The outcome, however, was not what he had anticipated. When he arrived, classes had already been going on for months because the Institute admitted its first group of applicants from every subject of study.

Despite the odds, Tesfaye chose to submit his application to the registrar. He eventually reached out to the Institute's director in person after bickering at the registrar's office.

The Institute's director, Ato Bekri Abdulahi, asked, *"How can I help you?"*

"You see, sir! I am really excited to continue my study at the polytechnic Institute. I satisfy all of the Institute's requirements."

"I got the highest scores on the national eighth-grade exams. I belong to this institute! Could you kindly help me with getting admission? These are my docs, please!"

Tesfaye begged modestly.

Ato Bekri answered, *"I'm sorry, but we can't admit you to the Institute at this time." "First of all, you weren't one of the students that were admitted to this Institute. Second, you have already missed many months' worth of lessons."*

"Therefore, there is no way we can admit you for this academic year," he said. After reviewing Tesfaye's academic credentials, he informed him, *"Sorry, I can't approve your application."*

Despite all the restrictions he had been outlining, Tesfaye did not relent and kept appealing to the director to let him in. He also assured the director that he would make every effort to try to compensate for the lessons he had to miss.

But it was all for naught; he failed. The director flatly refused to let him in.

Tesfaye persevered, though. He decided to remain at the hotel, make regular early morning appearances, and maintain his appeal to the director. The fact that Tesfaye persisted in his attempt for more than two months is astounding. He was so relentless that Ato Bekri and other Institute administrators had had enough of him.

Tesfaye noticed a glimmer of optimism around December. One fine day, Ato Bekri devised stringent requirements before agreeing to admit him.

"Hello, brave boy!" Ato Bekri greeted Tesfaye with a smile.

"*Well, it is incredible,*" he started.

"*Even though it has been months, you haven't stopped asking for entry. I'm giving your application more thought because of your bravery and dedication.*"

"*Here are the terms and conditions under which you would be given full entrance,*" he continued.

"*The final exams for the semester are scheduled for this month of December for the students. If you could take the semester final examinations with the regular students and receive a passing grade, the Institute will approve your candidacy.*"

"*Do you agree to this requirement?*" Ato Bekri asked inquiringly.

"*I do, yes!*" Tesfaye answered with assurance. He found the choice made by the Institute to be nearly unbelievable.

He was told by Ato Bekri, who was shaking his head incredulously, to study hard for his examinations.

He wished him luck and left.

Tesfaye sat for the final exams with the regular students even though he hadn't taken any of the lectures during the semester.

He understood the exam topic well, which helped him get top marks. He believed his future had been secured the instant he discovered he had done well on the exam.

His exceptional accomplishment astounded Ato Bekri and other local and foreign staff. And Tesfaye was instantly admitted to the Bahir Dar Polytechnic.

Tesfaye spent four years studying industrial chemistry (1964-67).

"Though I joined graduate school after graduating from Bair Dar Polytechnic Institute, I feel I had learnt not much since then," he said of his time at the Institute.

Bahir Dar Polytechnic Institute primarily made my further studies and accomplishments a lot easier.

Chapter 3: The Exposure to First Foreign Education

The Missed Scholarship Chance to the United States

Tesfaye earned a degree in industrial chemistry with great distinction from Bahir Dar Polytechnic Institute in 1967. His photograph with Emperor Haile Selassie, at the award ceremony, was taken down from the walls of his parent's home under the Dergue regime. The photo was taken down despite him being one of the two top graduates from the inaugural class of Bahir Dar Polytechnic Institute who was given a gold medal and a gold pen.

It is a momentous day in his life. On this occasion, he was given other possibilities in addition to the gold medal and pen that were presented to him by Emperor Haile Selassie.

Here's a brief account of what happened.

After being presented with the gold medal by the Emperor, Tesfaye was about to walk when he felt the Emperor's touch on his shoulder.

Tesfaye stopped and turned to face the Emperor, who asked, *"So, what is your next plan?"*

Tesfaye maintained his composure and told the Emperor, *"I have accepted a job offer from the Ministry of Labor and Social Affairs through*

H.E. Ato Getahun Tessema, Minister of Social Affairs, and I will begin working for them immediately."

"But this is not the time for you to be working," the Emperor said.

"Instead, now is the time to continue your further education. I thus want you to enroll in a foreign university and finish your further studies. You need to report right away to Ato Akalewold Habtewold! I'll instruct him to make everything easier."

"I will, Your Majesty!" Tesfaye replied courteously and walked away.

Tesfaye told the Emperor that the job offer had been made months before.

After interviewing Tesfaye and other brilliant students, Ato Getahun and his associates made the extraordinary offer for Tesfaye to join the Ministry as the Director of the Hawassa Oil Factory after graduation. Tesfaye had been in contact with the officials in the six months following his graduation after accepting the offer.

On the graduation evening, Tesfaye had another encounter with the Emperor. In honor of the occasion, a dinner party was held for him.

The Institute's hall hosted the ceremony. His beloved father, Aba Fira Biftu, was also invited.

Tesfaye still considers this to be one of his most fascinating and unforgettable life experiences.

Tesfaye was called out by name to receive another special award from the Emperor in the middle of the event. Ironically, he had missed hearing his name announced since he had not anticipated receiving an award a second time.

However, the announcer repeatedly called out his name. Upon hearing the announcement, his father, Aba Fira Biftu, abruptly sprang up and said, "Here I am!" He thought the announcer was summoning him.

"With great pride, I accepted an exceptional present from Emperor Haile Selassie and gave it to my father right away. Not only did I do it in response to my father's earlier statement, I firmly thought he deserved the medal.

Everyone who was there and watching the event was pleased with what I did. After keeping the prize for some time, my father later gave it to my youngest son, Beniam." Tesfaye recounts.

Tesfaye was summoned to the Ministry of Education, where he saw the Minister, Ato Akalewold, while Ato Getahun and his coworkers excitedly awaited Tesfaye to begin working as per their arrangement.

"Tesfaye, congratulations! You are given a scholarship chance to pursue your further study in the United States of America with the honorable endorsements of the Emperor. Ato Akalewold informed him that the application procedure could start right now."

Tesfaye reacted joyfully to the Minister, saying, *"I am really grateful for the scholarship. I'll start the preparation right now."*

As he was leaving the Minister's office, he thought about the position that the Minister of Labor and Social Affairs had given him. Even though he was thrilled to get the scholarship and had decided to begin the application process immediately, he thought it was his duty as a responsible person to let Ato Getahun Tessema know about the new news.

He went to the Ministry of Labor and Social Affairs to inform them about the scholarship and that he could not accept the job the Minister had offered.

He was welcomed warmly by the Minister, Ato Getahun Tessema, and the Minister of State, Bilata Nigatu Wolde Georgis.

"We were waiting for you to graduate so we could hire you to work with us. You're soon fortunate to be one of this government institution's youngest directors, the Minister said with a smile.

"I'm sorry, but I won't be able to start working for you right now. The Emperor's recommendation got me a scholarship for my higher studies. I'm currently applying to attend a university in the United States of America.

He said politely to the two, *"I hope I'll work with you someday when I return after graduating."*

None of the Ministers was pleased with his reply. The main reason was that the Minister of State, Bilata Nigatu, was schooled in French.

So, to sway his opinion, they pointed out the respect the French language enjoys and the advantages of attending a French university. On the other hand, they made him aware of how poorly American institutions performed academically.

The Minister advised him, *"So, you either enroll in one of France's top colleges or take a scholarship to study in the US and lose the chance to have quality education - the option is yours."*

Tesfaye was advised to quickly reject the scholarship offer in the US that he had already begun processing.

He was given a chance to attend a French institution on scholarship in exchange for agreeing to work for the Ministry of Labor and Social Affairs for a year.

He opted to forego the scholarship to pursue his higher education in the US since he was an ambitious and gifted young man determined to attend the best university.

Running the Hawassa Oil Factory and Reuniting With the Emperor

Tesfaye's first employment came after he agreed to the suggestion that he study in France; as a result, the Minister of Labor and Social Affairs nominated him as Director of the Hawassa Oil Factory, and he began that position in 1968. He was just sixteen years old when he was appointed as the Director of the plant.

Emperor Haile Selassie paid a visit to the factory while Tesfaye served as a Director. Tesfaye was the ideal guide for the trip. He was a little taken aback, but he wasn't sure the Emperor would know him. Ato Getahun, the Minister, was also a member of the hosting group traveling with the Emperor.

Tesfaye Biftu, with white gown, guiding
Emperor Haile Selassie, Hawassa oil factory

Tesfaye informed the guests about the oil factory's many products, its key accomplishments to date, and its future objectives while donning a white robe with the emblem of Bahir Dar Polytechnic InstituteEmperor, to his surprise, had remembered him and by the end of the visit, asked:

"Why did you refuse to continue your higher study in the US?"

The Emperor's recollection astounded Tesfaye, who responded that he was getting ready to embark on his studies overseas. Of course, he made no mention of the precise university he intended to attend. To share further information on Tesfaye's roles and potential future prospects, the Minister, Ato Getahun, personally attended the event.

Minister Getahun remarked, *"Your Majesty, Tesfaye has been rendering exemplary service. The success of the business is a result of his leadership. We'll see to it that he quickly pursues his higher studies overseas."*

Chapter 4: The Trip to France - Higher Education In Normandy

Caen University, Normandy

Tesfaye left the plant after a year to pursue his higher education in Paris, France. He was excited to continue studying his favorite subject at a higher level because, as promised by his supervisors, he had been looking forward to acquiring the highest quality education possible in France.

Despite his admiration for Paris, Tesfaye did not stay long. He was transferred to Caen University, located in Normandy, one of France's northernmost districts.

Normandy is a major producer of cider and calvados, a distilled cider or apple brandy.

Normandy was best renowned for its massive cattle and dairy industry when Tesfaye enrolled at Caen University.

It was a naturally beautiful location, but it was not as sophisticated in industrial technology as other parts of France. Overall, Tesfaye was underwhelmed by what he witnessed in Normandy.

Caen University in Normandy, founded by Henry VI in 1432, is one of France's oldest universities. Caen's main campus is historically significant. The institution was destroyed during WWII and rebuilt in the postwar period, including the main campus established in 1957.

When Tesfaye joined Caen University, it was one of the country's newly developed higher education institutions. Tesfaye attended Caen University's first-year programs, which focused on language and common courses as requirements for enrolling in a more specialized university.

He relocated to Paris after finishing his first year at Caen University.

The 1968 Paris Protests and the Tragedy of an Ethiopian Student

Following Tesfaye's admission to the university in Paris, another Ethiopian student relocated to the city for further studies. Protests erupted in Paris at the time. It was "May 1968," a day that some saw as a historic moment for social change, while others worried that traditional collective activity would end and anarchy would prevail.

Student protests against capitalism, materialism and conventional institutions, morals, and order were the catalyst for the unrest's start. It subsequently expanded to factories, with 11,000,000 workers striking for two weeks, representing more than 22% of France's total population.

The movement was distinguished by its impulsive and decentralized wildcat attitude, which provoked tension and, at times, conflict with the system, labor unions, and workers' parties. Its resounding cries of liberty, equality, and brotherhood had gripped human imagination.

The French had precipitated major transformations that had resulted in significant socioeconomic and political shifts worldwide. The French Revolution (1789-1799) was an era of political, ideological, and social upheaval in France and Europe that ended authoritarian dictatorship and welcomed new Enlightenment-based governmental structures.

The revolution was fought for liberty, equality, and brotherhood.

Tesfaye was present when university students ignited the Paris demonstrations. These protests quickly increased as general strikes extended to workplaces and industries nationwide. The transportation system had been shut down, and France appeared to be on the verge of a violent revolution.

An unlucky Ethiopian student who had lately arrived in Paris was met by demonstrators by the Seine River one day during a rally.

He appeared to be from middle east, and protestors attacked him, thinking he was an Algerian. The student from Ethiopia attempted to flee the gathering.

He did not, unfortunately, succeed. The protestors forced him into the Seine River, where he drowned. The enraged crowd was out to exact vengeance on anyone perceived as a French enemy.

Tesfaye was shocked by the murder of an Ethiopian student by protesters. Tesfaye's parents were devastated by the sad incident at home. He describes the tragic incident as follows:

"After a few days, news of the Ethiopian student's death reached Ethiopia. People in Ethiopia who heard the news were unsure who the victim was. Those who knew me assumed I was the student who was killed in Paris. My parents were also informed that I had been slain and directed to Bole AirPort to retrieve my remains. My parents were taken aback, which is understandable. Later, Ethiopian officials informed my parents that the student murdered in Paris was not me but another Ethiopian who had recently visited Paris. Despite their relief at the dreadful news being reversed, the episode had temporarily upset my parents and relatives. Once the protest ended, I discovered the lie regarding the Ethiopian student's death and its impact on my family."

Unfortunately, neither the French nor the Ethiopian authorities looked into the case of the Ethiopian student slain in a broad daylight. As a result, his killers were never brought to justice.

Tesfaye completed his study in Paris and was ignorant of any potential racial motivation for the murder until he had firsthand experience with the perils of racism.

Return to Addis Ababa on National Duty

To negotiate a bilateral agreement between Ethiopia and France for technical assistance, the Ethiopian State Minister, Bilata Nigatu Wolde Georgis, paid an official visit to Paris in 1970. Tesfaye was still a university student in Paris at the time.

The Minister and his colleagues had also convinced him to continue his education in Paris. During his visit, the visiting Minister expected to meet with Tesfaye.

Tesfaye was designated to accompany the Minister during his bilateral meetings with French government officials upon his arrival.

Taking Charge of the Bilateral Project

Bilata Negatu was delighted by Tesfaye's role in the mission's successful end and voiced his wish for Tesfaye to manage the project's conception and execution back home.

"I am glad to inform you," Bilatta Negatu stated, *"that your assistance was critical in winning the huge grant for our country's development." But we still need your help to start the project planning and implementation in Ethiopia. So, once again, I would like to ask for your assistance*

in assisting the project's start-up. You might help us for six months and then return to Paris to continue your degree!

The Minister asked, *"I hope you will use this opportunity to help your country."*

Tesfaye paused to consider the situation and concluded that he should not pass up the chance to benefit his country.

"I am sure I must accept the offer and am delighted to serve my country!" he told the Minister.

Tesfaye dropped out of college for six months and returned home to complete the mission entrusted to him. He was named project manager for the agreed-upon six-month period. Tesfaye was given an excellent villa, a vehicle, and all other necessities in Hawassa.

Tesfaye was successful in getting the project back on track after six months. He desired to return to Paris and continue his study. He, therefore, reaffirmed to Bilata Negatu Wolde Georgis that he had kept his word and wanted to return to Paris to finish his studies.

Conversely, the Minister asked Tesfaye to stay longer, saying, *"We still need your technical support until the project enters a reliable phase. Therefore, I advise you to work with us for a set period before returning to Paris."*

This time, Tesfaye was uncomfortable with the Minister's suggestion. He was dissatisfied by the Minister's failure to follow his commitment and, as a result, opted not to work any further.

He resigned and departed Hawassa for Addis Ababa the next day. He never even asked the office for a formal resignation.

Meeting With Congressman Paul H. Todd, Jr. and the Management of Ethiopian Spice Extraction Laboratory

Tesfaye could not return to France to finish his further study after quitting his job. But shortly after, he saw a job opening at one of the recently formed international businesses in Addis Ababa.

In 1970, American congressman Paul H. Todd, Jr. founded a small business named Ethiopian Spice Extraction Company in Ethiopia, not far from Addis Ababa. The company desperately needed a chemist who could work on the projected products' research and development.

Tesfaye had a substantial career in industrial chemistry and research. Thus he was eager to join the business. Fortunately, he applied for the opening and was accepted by the firm.

Tesfaye got to talk with Congressman Paul Todd after joining the firm when the latter visited the Ethiopian Spice Extraction Laboratory for a summertime inspection.

They discussed how research might increase the manufacturing output of the business's spice commodities. When Tesfaye joined the company, it barely operated at 80–90% of its extraction yield potential.

Congressman Paul Todd was involved in technological issues while being a politician at that time. Tesfaye's technical prowess caught the congressman's attention, and he decided to improvise with him. The congressman hoped to increase the extraction yield capacity and revenue significantly.

Tesfaye's performance greatly pleased US congressman Paul Todd. He was confident that the young man genuinely deserved the chance to advance his career and be in a position to make a significantly more significant contribution to the development of his nation.

Congressman Todd pledged to check into Tesfaye's options for a scholarship in the USA, and Tesfaye was motivated to pursue his dream of earning a higher degree.

Fortunately, Congressman Paul Todd soon secured a scholarship for the young researcher in one of the US state colleges. In 1972, Tesfaye signed up for Western Michigan University and began his undergraduate studies there.

In 1974, a left-wing military regime came to power in Ethiopia, and the corporation that extracted spices was nationalized in 1975.

In its case against Ethiopia in the US, the business demanded $11 million in compensation.

Furthermore, according to David Cary, an Associated Press (AP) correspondent in Nairobi, Kenya, in 1985, the Ethiopian government was prepared to pay $7 million in compensation to American corporations for assets nationalized following the 1974 revolution.

The company's president, Paul Todd, was described by the associated press report as saying, "We are totally satisfied, in light of the challenges in Ethiopia."

The report also said that several firms pursued 35 American compensation lawsuits against Ethiopia at one time in 1981. However, it is unknown how many of these claims were resolved.

Paul Todd and young Scientist Tesfaye collaborated on research on color extraction, and their findings were ultimately published in the prestigious scientific journal Journal of Food and Agricultural Chemistry in 1979.

Chapter 5: Higher Studies in the United States of America

American Society in the Early 1970s and the Massive Civil Rights Movement

In July 1971, Tesfaye enrolled at Western Michigan State University. Even though he had previously traveled overseas, he viewed the US as a well-developed nation overall.

Tesfaye had lived under two significantly different socioeconomic and political systems: the constitutional monarchy of Ethiopia and the then-advanced US system, defined by the excruciating fight of black people to overcome racial discrimination.

Significantly, the civil rights movement was a significant socio-political development when Tesfaye settled in the US. The civil rights movement of the 1960s included social activities in the United States that sought to abolish racial segregation and discrimination against black Americans and to win governmental recognition and protection of the constitutionally guaranteed citizenship rights.

Large-scale campaigns of civic resistance distinguished the movement. Between 1955 and 1968, nonviolent protests and civil disobedience led to rough conditions and intense discussions between activists and political leaders. To address the injustices experienced by African Americans, federal, state, and municipal governments, corporations, and communities frequently had to act quickly.

The Civil Rights Act of 1964, which outlawed discrimination in employment practices based on race, color, religion, sex, or national origin, was one of the significant parts of the bill passed during this period of the Civil Rights Movement.

It also ended racial segregation in public places like restaurants and hotels and the unfair execution of voter registration laws.

The Immigration and Nationality Services Act of 1965 significantly increased the number of immigrants from non-traditional Northern European and Germanic backgrounds who may enter the US.

The Voting Rights Act of 1965 restored and safeguarded voting rights. And the Fair Housing Act of 1968 outlawed discrimination in housing sales and rentals.

In the South, African Americans entered politics once more, and young people around the country were motivated to take action.

Racial prejudice and repression persisted in American society irrespective of the civil rights advances of the 1960s. Even after the Rev. martin Luther King, Jr. launched the Poor People's Campaign and President Johnson proclaimed a war on poverty in 1968, the country's wealth and income distribution increased inequality in the 1970s and 1980s.

Despite their agreement that desegregation had not significantly improved the lives of impoverished blacks, civil rights activists disagreed on the direction in which black development should go moving forward.

The Fast-Paced Eighteen Months Graduate Degree at Western Michigan University

Western Michigan University was established in 1903 and is a student-centered, discovery-driven, and internationally connected state university amongst America's more than 4600 higher education institutions.

The university offers 147 Bachelor's, 73 Master's, and 30 doctorate degrees in addition to one specialty degree course and many graduate-level certification programs. Seven degree-granting colleges provide the courses: Arts and Sciences, Aviation, Education and Human Development, Engineering and Applied Sciences, Fine Arts, Business and Health, and Human Services.

The university is situated in Kalamazoo, Michigan, one of the top 25 places in the nation for fresh college graduates.

Tesfaye registered as a chemistry student at the College of Arts and Sciences. He had previously spent a great deal of time studying and practicing chemistry to grasp his coursework smoothly. It also gave him time to work there and earn some money.

He remembers his experience at Western Michigan University as follows:

"At Western Michigan, I became a full-time student and a full-time worker. Mr. Karl R. Sandelin and Paul Todd, a Congress member, motivated, helped and inspired me in many ways. They were also covering all of my bills and paying for my education.

But even so, I could work more than eight hours daily since I had lots of time and was relatively comfortable with my courses."

Tesfaye could finish the prerequisites for his first degree more quickly because he had a good grip on the subject.

A BSc in chemistry usually takes four years to complete. General chemistry and mathematics are covered in the first and second years. In contrast, physical chemistry, quantitative analysis, biochemistry, organic chemistry, inorganic chemistry, and physical chemistry are covered in the third and fourth years.

Students were expected to research with professors and graduate students in addition to their coursework. Tesfaye could finish his degree requirements in an astoundingly short time—eighteen months—thanks to his intellectual prowess and prior undergraduate work.

His majors were mathematics and chemistry, while his minor was economics.

Tesfaye also completed his graduate studies, MSc in Chemistry and Statistics, at the Western Michigan University in a record-breaking four years, earning both his BSc and MSc degrees.

"During my undergraduate years, I studied chemistry alongside mathematics and successfully finished two majors at the same time," he explains.

"As a result, I made the decision to do the same for my graduate studies. I was sure that I wouldn't have any trouble with graduate-level chemistry studies. So, in the graduate program, I studied statistics together with physical chemistry," he remembers.

Tesfaye sometimes struggled even if he was content with his academic accomplishments. One of these incidents happened when he was a freshman at Western Michigan. He remembers it like this:

"One of the prerequisites for Western Michigan's undergraduate program was to participate in four different sports.

Students had to enroll in at least one credit every semester and finish the courses during their stay, with each of the four athletic categories earning one credit. Despite being a foreigner in the US, I chose to sign up for swimming during my first year, in 1971.

A few weeks into the first semester of studies, I began my swimming practice at the university's swimming pool. While swimming, I experienced intense abdomen pain and blacked out one day. Thankfully, the swimming instructor and other people saved me from drowning and brought me to a nearby hospital immediately."

"I was rushed to an emergency room with several medical tests. Later, it was discovered that my appendix had become infected, causing continuous discomfort that made me dizzy. My appendix's infected segment was surgically removed. I had to stay in the hospital for a few days to heal," Tesfaye recalls.

Tesfaye relished his time with Ethiopian students pursuing higher education at the same college. There were just five candidates from Ethiopia. Mekonnon and Degefe were graduate students at the university studying library science. Later, at Addis Ababa University, Ato Mekonnon was appointed chief 6-kilo campus librarian.

Every Friday, the five Ethiopian students would get together. They conversed in Amharic, exchanging opinions and knowledge on various Ethiopian-related subjects.

Together, these students also ate traditional Ethiopian food. Even though they were busy during the week, the five students all found inspiration during their Friday meetings. The gang was together for virtually the entire evening. They had delightful and joyful moments together as newly arrived Ethiopians with fresh recollections of their homeland.

Tesfaye was supposed to return to Ethiopia and work for Congressman Paul Todd's Ethiopian Spice Company after completing his education in the US. He was getting 22 to 24 credits per semester to pace up and return as soon as possible. He was working in the administration of the Spice Extraction Company, owned by Congressman Paul Todd, and taking the maximum number of classes every semester.

Tesfaye joined the company, which had its headquarters in Kalamazoo, Western Michigan, intending to expand his expertise and increase his income. He was therefore juggling a full-time job and his studies at the same time.

Nobody anticipated that the Imperial regime would fall in 1974 due to a violent revolution. Despite the catastrophic revolution's effects, the military administration seized the Ethiopian Spice Extraction firm as a cornerstone of its communist political philosophy. Therefore, Tesfaye had little choice but to continue his further studies in the US.

His Part in Martin Luther King's Tutorial Program

The early 1970s in the US were marked by the implementation of several civil rights measures approved by Congress in the 1960s to enhance African Americans' social and political standing. During this time, black Americans' educational experiences saw significant changes as more and more of the previously all-white institutions and universities began to admit them.

Martin Luther King's Tutorial Program, a recently developed program, was introduced in Western Michigan as a part of this process. The program aimed to offer tutorial assistance to African-American students who hadn't had a good education before admission.

Tesfaye was one of the few college students chosen by the program to mentor and encourage Afro-American students who were accepted into the institution. He gave extensive lectures to many learners alongside other selected students. This, in his memory, was one of his most outstanding achievements.

"Many African American students used to benefit from the tutorial help we offered in a variety of areas, including chemistry, physics, and mathematics. The majority of the students who received tutoring help did well in their academic endeavors. I grew close to them. Some invited me to their churches, while others welcomed me into their homes and introduced me to their parents."

Chapter 6: Post Graduate Studies at Brandeis University

Tesfaye made a remarkable effort by completing two undergrads and two graduate degree programs in only four years. His professors and other academic workers at Western Michigan were astounded by his extraordinary academic accomplishments. Congressman Paul Todd, who had supported Tesfaye through the entire procedure, remarked that Tesfaye's performance went above and beyond.

Tesfaye was set to complete his Ph.D. studies as quickly as possible, motivated by his outstanding accomplishments.

He was sure he would rise to the challenge because of his prior knowledge. While still a student at Western Michigan, he began looking for a prestigious university to get his Ph.D. After some research and contemplation, he went to Brandeis University.

"When I enrolled at Brandeis University in Waltham, Massachusetts in 1975, I already knew who I would study with to begin my PhD. One of the most esteemed academics in the discipline of chemistry, Professor Robert Stevenson, was the person I was looking forward to. Although I was aware that PhD candidates must complete required courses and other academic assignments before beginning to work on their independent research, I thought I had a solid case for being spared from some of these demanding processes. I may have been overconfident that I could begin working on my PhD dissertation right away without devoting more time to coursework because I had successfully and

thoroughly studied organic chemistry various prestigious facilities, and excelled there."

Brandeis University was established in 1948 and bore the name of the late Louis Dembitz Brandeis, a renowned associate justice of the United States Supreme Court, and the values of academic achievement and social justice he embodied.

With 107 students and 13 staff members present, coeducational sessions were launched in Waltham, Massachusetts, the location of the former Middlesex University.

Brandeis University expanded rapidly under the leadership of its founding president, Abram L. Sachar, for 20 years, becoming an important national and worldwide institution for research and education. The institution received Phi Beta Kappa accreditation in 1961, just 13 years after its foundation.

The institution maintained the extremely human scale of its teaching environment and its strong liberal arts foundation under each consecutive president, expanding in breadth and prestige.

Brandeis University and the Bahir Dar Polytechnic: Tesfaye's Attachment to the Two Institutions

In the summer of 1975, Tesfaye Biftu enrolled at Brandeis University to work on his organic chemistry Ph.D. Any Ph.D. applicant must complete coursework, which often takes one to two years, per the standard procedure.

The Ph.D. applicant must start their research once they have completed their prerequisite courses. The student must pass cumulative exams consisting of six different tests on topics they have not covered before.

A month had passed when Tesfaye went to Professor Stevenson's office and asked him to begin working on his study. The Professor had previously turned down Tesfaye's plea due to formalities.

He had remarked, *"I don't think you comprehend the current policies and practices of the university's PhD program. You must complete the curriculum for at least a year before having conversations about how and who you would do the study with. You can communicate with different professors and ultimately choose with whom to do the study only after completing the curriculum."*

Tesfaye pressed his demand anyway. *"Professor, I am aware of the university's established protocols and policies,"* he added.

"However, I can promise you that I am acquainted with the type of study needed at this level. During my two years in Michigan, I spent a lot of time working in organic chemistry-related laboratories and enterprises. With exclusively you in mind, I decided to pursue my PhD at Brandeis University."

Tesfaye was being persistent, so Professor Stevenson, thinking of a way to terminate the situation, came up with a research project, gave it to Tesfaye, and stated,

"You are supposed to clearly characterize the structures of this natural product and extract its constituents. If you are successful, I will guide you to the next level."

Tesfaye was subsequently assigned to one of Professor Stevenson's five labs, where his students were conducting research for their Ph.D. requirements or other research projects. Student and postdoctoral researchers were given laboratories depending on their skills and performance. Professor Stevenson used to sit adjacent to the office next to the first laboratory.

The best researcher was assigned to the first laboratory, the second in rank to the second lab, and so on. Tesfaye was posted to the fifth or final lab by Professor Stevenson.

Making a Name for Oneself as a Medicinal Chemist With a Green Thumb

Tesfaye immediately got to work on the project and finished his first job in two weeks. He extracted its constituents from a natural resin and characterized the structures of the natural substances.

"The chemical comprises a steroid with a highly complicated structure, but I was able to describe them in all the necessary forms." After completing the project satisfactorily, I turned it over to Professor Stevenson. The Professor was stunned," Tesfaye recalls.

The Professor was partly surprised because Tesfaye finished the assignment so quickly. And also because he thought the project would be too big for Tesfaye to undertake. He subsequently told Tesfaye that he had handed the task to a previous student, John Williams, who was then working at MIT laboratories, as part of his Ph.D. thesis, but that the student had failed to deliver after working on it for two years.

Tesfaye could begin doing his Ph.D. study, according to Professor Stevenson, who was finally happy. He assigned him another equivalent task, which Tesfaye completed in six months.

The Professor had transferred Tesfaye to a lab in the center at the start of the second assignment. Tesfaye was invited to work at Professor Stevenson's first laboratory after completing the second project successfully.

"I completed the full Ph.D. program in two and a half years due to my past extensive experience in organic chemistry. Under normal conditions, the same program would have taken four to six years." Tesfaye claims.

Tesfaye also worked at Brandeis as a graduate assistant. His positive feedback from the students he mentored reinforced his desire to pursue academic research.

Chapter 7: Tesfaye's Return to Ethiopia Amid Political Unrest

Political Crisis in Ethiopia After Revolution

In 1978, Tesfaye abruptly decided to return to Ethiopia just a few months after completing his PhD program at Brandeis University. At the time, Ethiopia was going through one of its worst political conflicts, which eventually erupted into a protracted civil war. Tesfaye had no plan to travel back to his native land under such terrible political unrest.

The military and a minority of the urban population were the main drivers of the Ethiopian Revolution, which was a true public movement. There was a strong desire for faster economic growth and more political engagement throughout the nation.

Without even holding a phony election or paying rhetorical respect to popular sentiment, the military dictatorship that overthrew Haile Selassie stymied these goals and forced the nation into "socialism" in the Soviet model.

The speech Mengistu Haile Mariam delivered at Revolution Square in Addis Ababa, during which he yelled out loud chants such as "Death to counterrevolutionaries!" marked the formal launch of his Red Terror campaign.

EPRP (Ethiopian People Revolutionary Party) must perish!" Mengistu publicly shattered three bottles filled with what seemed to be blood on the ground to demonstrate the gravity of the action that would be taken against the rivals as part of the Red Terror campaign against EPRP and other opposition parties.

On the evening of May 1, 1976, the Derg gave Kebele (local government) authorities the instruction to detain any young person they suspected of belonging to the EPRP under the guise of an anti-government demonstration.

The Red Terror culminated in one of the most violent atrocities in Ethiopian history. The lifeless remains of young people, laborers, and intellectuals who had died as a result of the Derg's Red Terror campaign covered the streets of Addis Ababa and other cities in 1977/1978.

The security forces of the junta murdered them in cold blood.

Amnesty International estimates that between 10,000 and 30,000 people were slain in the capital city of Addis Ababa alone over the two months from December 1977 to February 1978.

The One-Stone-Two-Birds Mission: Teaching at Addis Ababa University as an Assistant Professor

Tesfaye came back to Ethiopia when these dreadful political events engulfed the entire nation. The nation was governed by a semi-feudal government in 1972, six years before he left.

When he came home in 1978, the nation was ruled by a military dictatorship that had an irrational desire to usher in a socialist revolution while embroiled in a bloody civil war. Why did he make the decision to come home at such a trying time?

He explains the motivation behind the perilous trip back to Ethiopia in the following way:

"I went back to Addis Ababa in 1978, just after I finished my PhD studies. I didn't start out with this in mind. But because of the evident and impending life-threatening circumstance that my father had experienced, I was obliged to make the decision to assume the greatest danger to my life and return to Ethiopia. My father, who had been a constant throughout my life, was accused of possessing illegal weapons and imprisoned by the military administration."

The sad political incident mentioned above occurred while Tesfaye's parents were residing in Agaro. Tesfaye did, in fact, keep in touch with his father frequently when he was living in the US.

Every Saturday morning, he called his father and spoke with him. The weekly phone calls on Saturdays had benefited in keeping his family's affection and support and in boosting his self-assurance. The routine was broken one dreadful Saturday.

"I called my father's regular landline number 40, which I can still remember, to have a conversation. I was informed that he was not available to speak to me right away when I picked up the phone instead of hearing his customary voice full of affection. I should call again the following week, the person on the other end of the line recommended.

Even though I found the remark odd, I was forced to wait until the next Saturday. I finally called back after a tense seven-day wait. He wasn't around to speak to me anymore. Naturally, I made the assumption that something dreadful may have occurred this time. I begged everyone to let me know what was truly going on." Dr. Tesfaye recounts.

He added, *"My family did not want to let me know his precise whereabouts. Therefore, I was really concerned. And, of course, I was aware of the country's heinous political conduct. It was possible to kill anyone at any time. "I was eventually given another phone number to contact him,"*

He made a call without waiting around. The loud voice of a telephone operator answered the call and greeted the caller.

"Hello! Greetings, sir! I want to speak with Aba Fira." (Tesfaye was aware that in his neighborhood, his father was more often referred to as Aba Fira.)

The operator finally responded, *"Wait for a moment,"* and connected his father to the call.

"Hello, dad. How are you doing?" Dr. Tesfaye questioned in a trembling voice.

"Good morning, my child!" His father asked with compassion. Tesfaye was longing, *"How about you?"*

I'm doing well, Dad, although I was really concerned because we haven't spoken in the previous two weeks. Dad, where are you now? What has happened to you?

Then, in a startling voice, his father said, *"My son!"*

"Pay attention to what I say. I'm now being held in Kerechelle (a detention center). I was detained many weeks ago on suspicion of housing illicit firearms. They arrested me and are looking into the matter. Since they don't have any evidence to back up the claim, I'm hoping to be released shortly."

Tesfaye was stunned for a while before responding, *"Oh, Dad! I apologize deeply. I need to come right away and do everything I can to help!"*

"Please! I beg you, my kid! Do not even consider doing this! Don't come! Everything will work out well! Just remain patient and calm. Aba Fira pleaded.

"I am aware of what is going on in the country! But, whatever happens, I have to come and try to help!" Tesfaye answered. But the jail security guard interrupted them and ended the call.

Tesfaye has never experienced something so horrible in his life. He realized why his father forbade him from returning to Ethiopia.

Even though the Red Terror was coming to an end, there was no peace in the country. At that time, the military dictatorship routinely executed young people, and parents were cruelly made to foot the bill for the bullets that claimed their children's lives.

For Dr. Tesfaye, life without his father was unimaginable. Dr. Tesfaye started working on getting specific information regarding the accusations and the best ways to fight them as soon as he learned about the arrest.

He discovered while researching the case that Ato Mamo, one of his closest friends, and his father had both been taken into custody. Additionally, he discovered that Ato Mamo was murdered by Derg agents in front of his own children, purportedly as a result of illicit firearms being taken from his house.

Dr. Tesfaye was disturbed to learn about his father's close friend's execution.

"The security officers had searched my father's house for prohibited weapons, but they had turned up nothing. I was concerned that my father might suffer the same fate as Ato Mamo, though. After running through a lot of probable outcomes in this situation, I ultimately made the decision to meet my father before anything unfortunate happens and immediately started making arrangements to go back to Ethiopia," he says.

He decided to apply for a teaching position at Addis Ababa University while keeping an eye on his father's legal situation since he anticipated that his stay in the country would be longer. He was aware that the University was experiencing a staffing deficit in the academic field. Since the military had targeted intellectuals, life in Addis Ababa was perilous for them.

Though his personal safety would be at continual risk, he hoped that the institution would accept his application positively and that this would provide him a justification to remain in Ethiopia.

He sent a letter of recommendation from Brandeis University and his qualifications with his written application to teach chemistry in the Faculty of Science.

The Addis Ababa University administration was pleased with his application and quickly offered him the job. After the Addis Ababa University hiring procedure was complete, Dr. Tesfaye Biftu wasted no time and went to Agaro to speak with his father. He had gathered all pertinent facts on his father's case and condition.

Aba Fira couldn't believe his eyes when he saw his kid standing in the visitors' area of the jail.

"My son, why did you come?" He softly greeted him, *"Didn't I urge you to stay away?"*

Dad, don't worry! Everything will work out well! Dr. Tesfaye responded with trepidation.

After a few minutes, the two men sat down and began delving into the case. Although he had undergone a challenging interrogation, his father informed him that no proof had yet been discovered to back up the accusation.

Dr. Tesfaye's hope was slightly restored after seeing his father. And he resolved to do all in his power to win his father's release.

The First Graduate Chemistry Program at Addis Ababa

Soon after Dr. Tesfaye joined the university, he and his colleagues established the first Chemistry Graduate Program. The beginning of the master's program is referred to as a turning moment in the history of the Chemistry Department at Addis Ababa University, as described on the institution's official website. The Chemistry Department established a graduate program leading to an MSc degree in 1978.

It was a turning moment in the Department's history and a significant step toward meeting the nation's demand for highly qualified personnel. The Department's research capacity began to expand with the launch of the graduate program.

Consequently, several well-known research groups were established in the Department. The achievement of the MSc curriculum pushed the Department to begin a Ph.D. program as part of its training program. The original offering of the system adopted a "sandwich" plan in cooperation with reputable colleges across Europe with the ultimate goal of operating a complete in-house Ph.D. program.

Many applicants have already received their PhDs, while many more are still in the study process. The Department provides service courses to students of the School of Medicine, School of Pharmacy, Institutes of Technology, and other students of the College of Natural and Computational Sciences in addition to its regular curriculum. Additionally, the Department participates in a summer in-service course for educators that leads to a BSc in chemistry.

Originally known as the University College of Addis Ababa, Addis Ababa University was founded in 1950. It was elevated to a university in 1962 and named Haile Selassie I University. The institution's official website states that 33 students were enrolled in 1950.

This has grown to 48,673 students by 2014 (33,940 undergraduate, 13,000 graduate, and 1733 doctoral students). And there were now 6043 employees (2,408 academics and 3,635 support staff). The university presently offers diverse health science specialties throughout its 14 campuses through its 293 graduate programs (72 Ph.D. and 221 Master's) and 70 undergraduate programs. Due to the "development through partnership campaign," Addis Ababa University was shuttered in post-revolution Ethiopia for two years.

Dr. Tesfaye made a substantial contribution to the improvement of the Chemistry Department's research capabilities at Addis Ababa University. He was able to create and carry out action research programs to solve the crucial needs of Addis Ababa University in medicinal chemistry and related fields because of his outstanding research capacity and significant experience in the renowned medical chemistry facilities in the United States.

"During my brief time at the University, I realized that, despite the fact that there were a few researchers in the area, facilities, experiences, and priorities for research in medical chemistry. As a result, I made the decision to form small research groups as part of the graduate program,

in addition to assisting in the establishment of the MSc program in chemistry.

In order to determine the ability, resources, and possibilities for doing research in the real-world environment of the institution and the nation, I started an investigation with colleagues. Then, we started conducting research in natural products and electro organic synthesis. We picked the most important areas of study after determining the current capability and available resources through the survey."

If the Derg administration, which sought cooperation with nations associated with the Soviet Union, had not resisted such ideas and opposed connections between US science universities and Addis Ababa University at the time, Dr. Tesfaye would have been able to enable those connections.

After more than 70 years of friendship, Ethio-US relations broke down during the Derg government. Political and commercial ties grew steadily following the formalization of diplomatic ties in 1903. After a summit in Egypt in 1944, relations between the US and Ethiopia improved. By 1974, Ethiopia's coffee exports had increased significantly, and the US had established itself as a vital source of military and economic assistance.

Dr. Tesfaye's return to Ethiopia took place at a crucial juncture in the bilateral relationship between Ethiopia and the US.

The US ended this connection and stopped providing any aid to Ethiopia. As a result, Dr. Tesfaye was compelled to give up his scheme to establish relationships between AAU and US colleges. The regime also believed he was working on a secret mission for the US government.

He wasn't aware for a long time that he was being kept under close observation by government security officials.

The Threat That Evolved Into a Welcome Opportunity and the Undercover Cadre

Dr. Tesfaye worked on his primary mission in Ethiopia and his duties at Addis Ababa University.

In particular, he was looking into realistic solutions to free his father from prison.

He regularly visited Agaro, and a few months after his return to Ethiopia, he was encouraged by the knowledge that his father was not the subject of any proof.

He had been talking with attorneys, family, and other people he felt would be able to advise him on some practical next steps. Nobody could do anything because the military government's security forces, not the courts, were in charge of the case.

He had no choice but to wait while keeping his eyes and ears open.

But then something started to happen one day. He recalls the entire incident as follows:

"I still recall the day I was in the university's scientific lab with my coworker Dr. Berhanu Abegaz. As we started working on the chemistry project in the lab, we talked about a few things. Berhanu Abegaz abruptly asked, "Frankly, I do not yet comprehend the purpose of your return to Ethiopia. When Ethiopia was engulfed in such terrible political strife, why and how did you decide to return? Could you explain what brought you back home while we are all frantically looking for ways to leave this unstable and war-torn nation?"

Dr. Tesfaye admits, *"I was not startled by his statement. His question was rational and clear. I said, "I was aware of the prevalent volatility and insecurity in this nation," after a little pause. I had to go back to Ethiopia, though.*

My father was imprisoned by government security personnel a few months ago because he had illegal firearms stored in his house. While monitoring his case from afar, I discovered that he was dealing with a grave scenario. I've always had a close bond with my father.

His assistance has been crucial to my overall academic achievement. Life without him is unimaginable to me. That is why I decided to go back to Ethiopia and do whatever I can to support him," he said.

What a heartbreaking story! Exclaimed Dr. Berhanu Abgaz after being moved by the tale. "Have you rescued him?" he questioned.

Dr. Tesfaye answered, "Not yet. I have a few people I felt would be helpful. But none of them has offered a workable solution. Nothing can be done but wait, he said.

While acknowledging your bravery, Dr. Berhanu Abegaz continued, "I should warn you to be careful and, as you said, look for practical ways.

I hope you realize how quickly the military government may act these days foolishly," he said.

Dr. Tesfaye responded, "Yes, I understand it very well, and I appreciate your counsel.

A man was listening to the entire talk as Dr. Tesfaye was narrating his tale to Dr. Berhanu Abegaz; Leykun Jemaneh. He was a biology student at the university's 4-kilo campus. In addition, he was one of the military regime's cadre and ardent supporters. Leykun had been secretly watching Dr. Tesfaye's every move since he returned to Ethiopia and, more precisely, ever since he started working at AAU. National security services had Dr. Tesfaye under close observation because they thought he might be a covert spy for the US government.

Leykun greeted Dr. Tesfaye as he exited the lab and said, *"Excuse me, but I heard the narrative you told Dr. Berhanu Abegaz! This tale is heartbreaking. Look! About your father, don't worry.* He said softly, *"I might be able to help you find a way out."*

Then, with assurance, he boldly handed Dr. Tesfaye a red card he had taken from his pocket and said, *"Here, Dr. Tesfaye! I work for the government. I'll do everything I can to assist you."*

Dr. Tesfaye Biftu felt conflicting emotions in response to what Leykun had said. The offer from Leykun was impressive but also a little alarming.

Dr. Tesfaye said, "This is unbelievable, but thank you so much for your kindness and willingness to help me.

Leykun had already seen Dr. Tesfaye before, but he was ignorant of his covert objective. They frequently shared coffee and spoke about multiple threads.

Dr. Tesfaye first interacted with Leykun at AAU, just as he met many other students. Unlike other professors at AAU, Dr. Tesfaye was eager to build cordial relationships with his students. He loved having coffee with his students and used to enjoy open discussions about numerous topics.

Leykun was someone he got to know at the Science Faculty in Arat Kilo, and they frequently drank coffee together at the local Tourist Hotel. But no one could have ever thought Leykun would be a covert spy.

Only until he unmasked himself and showed Dr. Tesfaye his ID card did the latter discover that he had been spying on him all since his return from the US and induction at AAU.

The incident showed what type of danger Dr. Tesfaye had taken by going back to Ethiopia. There was no going back on that decision.

Tesfaye's priority was his father's release. And in this regard, he had to choose how to react to Leykun's offer. He gave it some serious thinking. At last, he made up his mind and decided to deal with Leykun very carefully.

Dr. Tesfaye inferred from his chats with Leykun that the military administration had concluded that his return to Ethiopia had little to do with any secret US operations. Dr. Tesfaye struggled to develop a plan of action since he was motivated to use this knowledge as effectively as possible. Fortunately, he just needed to do a little when one lucky morning, Leykun came.

"I honestly didn't think Leykun would be of assistance, yet he somehow honored his promise. He handed me a letter from the nation's president, Colonel Mengistu Haile Mariam, requesting my father's release from custody. The letter, which demanded his immediate release, was written to the administration of the Jimma zone. The release order had been issued by none other than Colonel Mengistu himself," Dr. Tesfaye recalls. *"My father had been held for a very long time on unproven allegations."*

Dr. Tesfaye couldn't understand how the security guard took the letter away from the nation's lawmakers and lawbreakers. How did everything take place?

The Primary Mission in Ethiopia Accomplished

After getting the letter from the office of Colonel Mengistu Hailemariam, Dr. Tesfaye Biftu wasted no time in arranging his father's release from the infamous military jail. So, the following day, he took an Ethiopian Airlines flight to Jimma.

"When I first got to Jimma, I went right to Captain Tesema Belay's office, who at the time served as the province's top administrative office. After a few ups and downs, I finally managed to meet him in his office, where I gave him the letter without having to give him any extra context as to why I was there," claims Dr. Tesfaye.

After carefully reading the letter for several minutes, the top administrator silently observed Dr. Tesfaye.

"Could you please stay outside for a while?" he said after a little pause.

Dr. Tesfaye left the office feeling a little perplexed and concerned. During the Red Terror campaign, the top administrator, Captain Tessema Belay, was notorious for his violent behavior. In case the letter was a forgery and Leykun was working against him, Dr. Tesfaye wondered what might transpire.

Nobody could entirely depend on the military government's security personnel. He lacked concrete proof that the president's administration issued the letter. He got tense because of these unsettling thoughts.

Captain Tessema Belay summoned him back to his office, much to the relief of Dr. Tesfaye, and read the letter aloud before responding, *"I will see to it that your father is released soon. The drivers will be instructed to transport you to Agaro on my orders."*

Dr. Tesfaye thanked everyone. It was now apparent that Leykun's gesture of support was sincere.

Captain Tessema Belay set up a military truck with a few security soldiers, as he had promised. Soon after, Dr. Tesfaye was transported to Agaro, a town 42 kilometers from Jimma city, where his father had been detained for several weeks.

When he reached Agaro, where his father was being held, he went to the prison's administration and asked for his father's release under the order. As Tesfaye arrived, he was told that Captain Tesema Belay had already spoken with all the case-related officials about the order of the release.

Dr. Tesfaye inquired if he might meet his father during the officials' discussion of the problem. He was permitted to go to a location designated for visitors to see convicts, where he met his father.

He welcomed him and exclaimed, *"Hello, Dad!"* with a smile. *"Thank God, you will soon be set free!"*

Aba Fira was shocked and asked, *"My son, why do you say so? Have you heard any hopeful news?"*

Dr. Tesfaye told his father about the letter. But in the middle of their discussion, Dr. Tesfaye received a call from the administrator's office. So, with the expectation that his father would be released immediately, he went to the administrator's office. However, he was merely given the information that his father would be released in a few weeks and that he could return to his job.

Dr. Tesfaye was upset. He questioned why it was not possible since he wanted to see his father released right away.

"Releasing your father right away while you are still here in Agaro might raise suspicion in the neighborhood that we were bought off to free your father," the administrator retorted.

They could believe that the *Adaharian* boys (children of counter revolutionaries) were rigging the court system with their wealth to get their parents out. Your father will soon be released soon after you return to Addis Ababa and resume working.

Dr. Tesfaye was not persuaded and requested an immediate release following the letter's instructions. The administrator was adamant that a quick release would undermine public trust and would not budge.

It was ludicrous because the military administration routinely and unilaterally violated the law. Dr. Tesfaye Biftu was left with no other option. He had to return to Addis Ababa because he was concerned that his father would remain imprisoned indefinitely.

Finding the Right Match

Dr. Tesfaye had spent one year and ten months in the University's Chemistry Department. Despite being brief, the time was still pivotal in many ways for him.

As planned by the administrator of the Agaro jail, Aba Fira was released from custody after a couple of weeks. It is one of the most significant accomplishments in Dr. Tesfaye's life. He thinks he succeeded in three main goals during his brief visit:

"The first and most significant accomplishment I made during my brief time in Ethiopia was getting my father out of jail."

"Yes, I successfully completed my main objective in Ethiopia, and my father was freed from jail after fulfilling the requirements set by the prison's administrator. This was one of my life's proudest moments."

"We had an incredible time together when my father subsequently visited my family in the US," Dr. Tesfaye recounts.

The start of the graduate chemistry program in the Science Faculty at Addis Ababa University was Dr. Tesfaye's second accomplishment during his time in Ethiopia. He played a crucial part in its establishment.

Few of Tesfaye's students, who were among the first postgraduates to enroll in the program, completed their Ph.D. programs in the USA and Australia and are now employed by top-tier companies.

His third accomplishment was meeting his beloved wife at this time.

How did they meet, and when?

Biology instructor Miss Tersit Taddasse worked at Akaki High School (a town near Addis Ababa). At the time, Addis Ababa University was hosting a summer program for teachers from various high schools around the country to advance their education and careers. Tersit Taddasse was one of the instructors in the biology department's summer program.

"I was her summer programme instructor. I quickly discovered that Tersit had the charisma and everything else that I most appreciated."

Even now, he remembers her as a person who was highly devoted, diligent, and trustworthy.

"The summer program ran from July through August. I participated in the summer program from 1978–1979. After finishing the summer program in 1979, I decided to tell Tersit what I had been thinking and feeling. I went up to her one day and asked if we could have some coffee and speak. She wasn't shocked when I invited her because we got along well.

She agreed to meet with me, and we talked about various topics. We quickly became good friends," recalls Dr. Tesfaye.

It didn't take long for the two to get to know one another's personalities and goals in life. It wasn't long before they decided to live together as partners.

They stayed together for another year while Dr. Tesfaye was there. For both of them, it was a tremendously motivating and productive period.

"We started making plans for our new position as soon as we decided to be married. After doing that, I returned to the USA exhilarated and inspired. I asked the US authorities to let my future wife visit the country right away. We were married in the US in 1981 after my request was accepted," Dr. Tesfaye recalls.

Mother Eleni Estifanos and father Taddasse Mengesha welcomed Mrs. Tersit into the world at Ras Desta Hospital in Addis Ababa. She has three siblings: Tsega-Selassie, Fekade-Selassie, and Hirut-Selassie Taddesse. Her mother was from Harar, while her father was from Menz. Currently, the siblings are all residing in the US.

During the reign of Emperor Haile Selassie, her father served as Chief of Justice and Afe-negus (roughly, "spokesman of the king") of the upper court for an extended period. Her mother worked as a teacher at Addis Ababa's prestigious Etege Menen School. Amazingly, her mother was a native speaker of six distinct languages. She had a command of English, French, Italian, Swedish, Afan Oromo, and Amharic

Afenegus Tadesse Mengesha with Chief Justice Burger of USA, Rome, 1958

W/o Eleni Estifanos

Mrs. Tersit acknowledges how her parents' moral compass has beautifully defined her personality. Her parents taught her to value her family, work hard, be humble, and be honest.

She says she has lovely memories of her youth. She enjoyed her time at Addis Ababa's Menelik High School. When she was younger, she wanted to become a lawyer like her father. But she went to Addis Ababa Teachers College to study biology and worked as a teacher.

She was a biology instructor at Akaki Secondary School in Akaki and Atse Fasil Secondary School in Gonder. It makes her happy to know that several of her former students have earned MDs and PhDs.

Dr. Tesfaye and Tersit, coincidentally, share a common ethnic and familial heritage. The father of Mrs. Tersit is an Amhara from Menz, while the mother is an Oromo from Harar. Dr. Tesfaye Biftu's mother is from Wollo, while his father is an Oromo from Illu Abbabor.

"Regardless of the benefits of this commonality in our ancestry, race was never a concern when we first met." Dr. Tesfaye exults, *"Nor has it ever happened during our later lives.*

Afenegus Taddasse Mengesha, Mrs. Tersit's father, was a well-known Chief of Justice under Emperor Haile Selassie. He received high praise for his impartiality, honesty, independence, and bravery while serving as the top judge in the country.

Chapter 8: How Does It Feel to Be a Globally Recognized Medicinal Chemist?

The Best Pharmaceutical Company in the World: Merck and Co.

When Dr. Tesfaye returned to the United States in 1981, he joined Merck & Co. Inc., one of the biggest pharmaceutical firms in the world. Merck gave Dr. Tesfaye a fantastic opportunity to showcase his extraordinary talent. He eventually became a renowned expert in the field of medicinal chemistry.

The corporate headquarters of the American pharmaceutical firm Merck & Co., Inc. is in Kenilworth, New Jersey (known as MSD outside of the US and Canada). The business was created in 1891 as the American division of the German corporation Merck, which was founded in 1668. During World War I, the US government took control of Merck & Co., which became an independent American corporation in 1917.

The company's history demonstrates that, since its founding, it has seen tremendous organizational development. Merck became the most prominent US pharmaceutical company in 1953 after partnering up with Philadelphia-based Sharp & Dohme, Inc., established in 1845 by Alpheus Phineas Sharp and Carl Friedrich Louis Dohme. The acquisition brought together Sharp & Dohme's sales and distribution network and marketing experience with Merck's scientific research and chemical manufacturing strengths.

Merck announced in November 2009 that it would combine with competitor Schering-Plough in a $41 billion merger. For Schering-Plough to formally remain as the surviving public firm, Merck was renamed Merck Sharpe & Dohme, and «Merck & Co., Inc.» was added to Merck.

The action was taken in an effort to protect Schering-marketing Plough's rights to Remicade, and arbitration was used to reach a result. The merger was completed on November 4, 2009.

Merck is currently a multinational corporation whose core activities include identifying, developing, producing, and selling goods and services to preserve and restore health. The business is a pioneer in innovative healthcare and is dedicated to enhancing health and well-being worldwide.

The company's primary products include diabetes, cancer, vaccinations, and acute hospital care. The business is still concentrating its research on diseases including cancer, hepatitis C, cardio-metabolic illness, infections with antibiotic resistance, and Alzheimer's disease, among today's most serious health concerns. It also leads the charge against newly developing infectious diseases and, most importantly, pandemics.

Tesfaye had a wonderful opportunity to harness his ability and achieve remarkable things after joining Merck. Even at the peak of his achievements, Tesfaye never lost sight of those who had assisted him in reaching his full potential. His mentor and sponsor, Congressman Paul Todd, who provided him with valuable support during his college and graduate studies, can never be forgotten.

So, soon after beginning his career at Merck, Dr. Tesfaye wrote the Congressman a heartfelt letter of gratitude.

The Congressman was delighted and said as such in response to the letter:

"No letter I have received in the last months has brought me such joy as yours! Hearty congratulations on your new job at Merck. You have fought for a very long time, and I am impressed by your tenacity, perseverance, and commitment. It's because of this that you survived. Now that you have this knowledge, you may continue your academic study of chemistry and potentially improve your personal and family relationships."

When Dr. Tesfaye joined Merck in 1981, there were hardly any Senior level black Americans working in medicinal chemistry. African Americans were not actively participating in their country's economic, or scientific life during this time. In the history of this prestigious organization, only Dr. Tesfaye and few African Americans had attained a relatively high position.

Dr. Tesfaye has worked on researching medications at Merck to treat conditions like obesity, metabolic disorders, infectious illnesses, immunological diseases, thrombosis, inflammation, and asthma. He has, individually or in collaboration with other medicinal chemists, received more than 100 patents for his drug discovery.

His contributions to Merck & Company have been so significant that he has often been given letters of gratitude and prizes in stock options.

Amazingly, Dr. Tesfaye played a crucial role in bringing Dr. Stevenson, a professor at Brandeis University, to Merck as a colleague. He persuaded Merck to appoint Professor Stevenson as an advisor, and the organization agreed.

Tesfaye then hired Professor Stevenson for a more senior role while he was the Senior Director of a Boston-based business founded with other former colleagues from Merck.

Attending Rutgers University for MBA in Business Management

Tesfaye grew increasingly conscious of the importance of management for his professional advancement while working at Merck. Plus, he was quite impressed by his father for his business expertise and was inspired by him to diversify his academics.

He eventually opted to enroll in the Rutgers University extension program to acquire an MBA.

According to Tesfaye, *"in order to grow in my field, I believed that I would need to study either law or business administration in my spare time. I eventually decided to pursue business administration at Rutgers University because I believed it would be more relevant to my future personal and corporate developments."*

Even though he was in the evening program, he recalls that the entire study gave him wonderful and unforgettable memories. Above all, he'll never forget one of the most helpful management classes he took as part of his MBA degree. Here's how he recollects his experience:

Furthermore, each group would designate its members as President/Chair, HR Manager, Finance Manager, Marketing Manager, and other positions to be responsible for each of its parts.

The course was taught across two semesters, so each member of the group should have taken on all of the positions provided by the corporation one by one and practiced various managerial duties.

"The chairperson and all other roles were rotated among the group members, and the teacher assigned regular assignments to the teams and remarked on each member's progress."

Furthermore, the groups presented their company's accomplishments and problems in the form of a report by a representative from each area. *"Despite the fact that most of the courses were given through case studies, Inter-functional Management was the most practical and, as a result, a memorable course to me,"* Tesfaye adds.

Challenges at Merck

Dr. Tesfaye says the following about his move to the United States and his time working for Merck: *"The United States of America has given me the freedom that I didn't have in my place of birth, Ethiopia. I had the freedom to live my life as I pleased and could raise my family in a free country."*

Even though Dr. Tesfaye had never faced obstacles when doing scientific research; race suddenly became a problem at Merck. Dr. Tesfaye discovered a drug (clinical candidate) called L-103 soon after he joined the firm in 1981. He finished the finding while adhering to all guidelines and regulations.

However, Merck eventually asked to transfer further studies to a white American scientist, Dr. WH, to follow up the drug he had identified. Dr. Tesfaye was baffled as to why the firm had given his invention to a different scientist when he, the inventor, was in the most significant position to take it to the next stage. Up until that point, it was customary for Merck to develop inventors of drugs alongside their products.

He eventually learned the secret of the medicine's development from Dr. Milt Hammond, a friend and fellow employee at Merck who was a candid and outspoken fellow.

Hammond explained, *"As a foreigner, you might not be aware of the racial politics in the US. Due to the prevalent racial politics, the* corporation is acting out of fear of losing money. The business is concerned that it could suffer a financial loss. Even if Merck acknowledges your discovery, if a black scientist like you developed the drug, it would not be accepted on the market. To guarantee the invention's adoption on the market, the corporation assigned a white scientist to the invention's development stage."*

Dr. Tesfaye was distraught by his colleague's explanation. He says the following about the incident:

"I found it insulting, despite Dr. Hammond's advice that I accept this as a reality in the US. I had never experienced racial prejudice, so I found it hard to imagine that I would lose my own finding just because of my ethnicity. It is true that, at the time, the practice was prevalent in the US. But when I was pursuing my further education in the country, I had not experienced such a challenge. Throughout my career as a medicinal chemist, this was among the most difficult situations I had ever encountered."

A similar racial dilemma arose a few years later, which Dr. Tesfaye never forgets. By performing an in-depth study on several natural items in 1985, he and his group discovered the asthma clinical candidate MK-287 from a lead compound Dr. Tesfaye made for his PhD program at Brandeis. Yet again, the business was assigned to another white scientist, Dr. JC to develop the product.

Dr. Tesfaye once more questioned the company's decision to entrust the second round of development of his invention to a different medicinal chemist. This time, the business may have been more circumspect in its approach since any instance of racial prejudice would have had dire legal repercussions for Merck. The corporation may have been sued since several civil rights protections were put in place.

The business representatives made the following arguments in an attempt to convince him:

'The follow up and development of such a medicine is best carried out by an American with a native accent to present and defend the finding, but your accent is African, as a result of which we might face critical challenges in the development and marketing of the product.'

They concluded that Merck decided to work with a different scientist during the development phases for practical reasons. However, Dr. Tesfaye knew that the true cause had little to do with his accent, which was a relatively small problem compared to a significant medical discovery.

At the time, Merck employed high-ranking white professionals with accents from Scotland, Greece, and other eastern and western European countries. It was Merck's tradition to develop scientists alongside their discovered products.

His Contribution to Medicinal Chemistry at CytoMed Inc.

Dr. Tesfaye Biftu joined CytoMed Inc., a start up reputable pharmaceutical business headquartered in Cambridge, Massachusetts, after working for Merck for 12 years. He hoped to fulfill his ambition of becoming a renowned scientist, and CytoMed appeared to provide better opportunities.

CytoMed is a biopharmaceutical business creating new medications to treat inflammatory illnesses. CMI-977, an oral drug for treating asthma, and CMI-392, a drug for treating inflammatory skin problems, were the two compounds the business had in clinical development.

CytoMed was completing the two medicines' development when Dr. Tesfaye Biftu joined the business in 1993. To do this, it partnered with significant pharmaceutical firms.

When Dr. Tesfaye worked for CytoMed, he held the Senior Director of Medical Chemistry position, overseeing several American and Asian scientists.

He made a significant contribution to the growth of CytoMed and the field of medicinal chemistry in general. He recalls that in CytoMed, he focused on three mediators; Nicotinic receptor agonists, Leukotrienes and Platelet Activating Factor.

Within a relatively short period of time, Dr. Tesfaye Biftu made a significant contribution to the growth of CytoMed. His style of leadership was creative and placed a high value on cooperation. The organization named him "Scientist of the Year" in 1993 to recognize his exceptional and distinctive achievements.

Dr. Tesfaye's employment at CytoMed was under two years (1993-1994). Tom Salzmann, vice president of Merck Executives of Merck & Co. extended him a second invitation back to Merck and promoted him in 1995 to Senior Investigator.

Back at Merck Pharmaceutical Company

The importance of Dr. Tesfaye's contribution to the company's expansion was recognized by Merck Company management, which was later validated. Dr. Tesfaye's friend and coworker, Dr. P. Liberator, says the following about his time at Merck and his return:

"Tes is very soft-spoken, not always the first choice to sell a project's successes. It is not just his personality. The number of people that seek

his opinion has been impressive, and I expect that to continue growing. In addition to the significant merger with Schering, Merck has undergone many restructuring and layoffs over the past ten or more years. Because of this, Tes's peers are no longer employed at Merck.

The fact that he stayed a Merck employee during this upheaval and uncertainty is evidence of his past, present, and future accomplishments."

Tesfaye has contributed to the discovery of more than 100 patents for candidates for medications, either working alone or in collaboration with the teams. Most of these discoveries were acquired after his 1995 comeback to the company.

Tesfaye has held several important leadership positions, including Senior Investigator from 1994 to 2005, Distinguished Senior Investigator from 2005 to 2012, Principal Scientist and Director of Discovery chemistry until he retired and left Merck in 2016. His impact in the global medicinal chemistry field has grown with his career inside the organization.

Tesfaye is regarded as one of the best medicinal chemists and travels widely to lecture and participate in several national and international symposiums. He has given lectures at the esteemed Pasteur Institute in Paris, France, international meetings in Florence, Italy, as well as at other universities and institutions in England, Sweden, and Portugal.

His old Merck coworker, Dr. P. Liberator, shares the following statement in this regard:

"I'm trained as a biologist, and Tes is trained as a chemist. We originally worked together on a drug development project 17 years ago while we were both working for Merck. Tes was always eager to spend the time necessary to address my naïve questions concerning medicinal chemistry and the methods used to direct the project. We probably only

collaborated on the project for four years, but we have kept up our working connection. Tes never stopped teaching me the subtleties of medicinal chemistry and giving me advice, regardless of the project we each went to.

Tes has worked on several successful initiatives throughout the years, but because of his modest nature, he often didn't get as much credit for his contributions. Tes is a fantastic instructor with a wealth of knowledge and a willingness to impart his exceptional understanding of the courses on medicinal chemistry."

Despite his outstanding contributions and amazing accomplishments, Dr. Tesfaye hasn't been given the role he deserves at Merck. Dr. Tesfaye was not bothered by this, according to his former coworkers.

He loves using persuasiveness to gain influence. He would have been immediately promoted to a senior leadership position if he had received the same treatment as other great white candidates. Dr. Tesfaye is aware that race is the main factor contributing to this.

"I think the African American battle against racial discrimination is far from over in the United States. America is a country where paradoxes are a way of life. Although there are many chances for people to improve their life, there are also significant racial obstacles. The privileges now enjoyed by Caucasian citizens are not the same by African Americans. However, I think that improving the situation is only a matter of time, possibly a prolonged spell. Merck's CEO and board chairman were white Americans when I started working there in 1981. It changed when African American attorney Kenneth Frazier was appointed board chairman and CEO in 2016. The fact that I got to see this event, a symbol of a big shift, makes me extremely happy," Tesfaye says.

Change, however, takes time, as the incident that follows shows. Marizev™, a brand-new once a week oral medication for diabetes was discovered by Dr. Tesfaye Biftu. According to the company's established norms and procedures, any medicinal scientist who leads successfully and has a track record as impressive as Dr. Tesfaye is most likely to advance to the position of a Vice President in the organizational hierarchy. Unfortunately, Dr. Tesfaye was not given that chance.

Chapter 9: The Settlement of an Ethiopian American Family in the United States

The Prosperous Scientist & Home-Maker: Mrs. Tersit Taddasse

Tersit-Selassie Tadesse

In addition to being a top-notch scientist, Dr. Tesfaye is a superb and ideal family man. The union he formed with Mrs. Tersit was prosperous. She completed her studies quickly and became a successful microbiologist in the US, as Tesfaye had said she would. She also rapidly adjusted to new surroundings.

Soon after relocating to the US with her devoted husband, Dr. Tesfaye, Mrs. Tersit enrolled in New Jersey's Kean University and quickly earned a BA in biology. She continued her education after that, enrolling at Seton Hall University in New Jersey to pursue a Master's degree in microbiology.

The institution not only allowed her to successfully concentrate on microbiology and get to know the diverse US culture, but it also gave her the chance to work as an assistant instructor in the biology department laboratory while she was still a student. It demonstrates how quickly she became used to the American educational system and flourished in her coursework.

Mrs. Tersit Taddasse claims that her success during her studies and later would not have been possible without the help of her devoted husband, Dr. Tesfaye. She explains his support as follows:

"It would have been quite challenging for me to complete my education without the valuable support of my beloved husband, Tesfaye. Tesfaye is a multidisciplinary scholar with extensive expertise in various disciplines.

He has been expertly tutoring me in various areas, such as mathematics, physics, genetics, and others, in addition to chemistry."

After earning a degree in microbiology from Seton Hall University, she worked as a laboratory assistant at a Boston-based children's hospital. The hospital was doing microbial research in collaboration with Harvard University. She now had a one-of-a-kind opportunity to progress her career by researching pediatric research.

After her family relocated to New Jersey, she worked on the development of several medications for various esteemed pharmaceutical firms. She spent 12 years working for Merck with eminent clinicians, pharmacists, and other experts. She has also worked with respected pharmaceutical firms, including Novartis, Esai, and Bayer.

She currently has extremely specialized knowledge and expertise in medication development and data management.

She maintains a positive outlook on America and its inhabitants, portraying them as benevolent and helpful people. Despite the system's evident flaws, she claims,

"I have seen in practice that Americans believe in helping others and giving them equal opportunity, regardless of other variables."

Mrs. Tersit retired early in 2015 to focus on other family tasks.

"I have a strategy to create smaller initiatives that will benefit Ethiopia's vulnerable and underprivileged populations. Hopefully, the initiatives will be put into action soon," she said.

One such admirable project of Mrs. Tersit strives to assist underprivileged pregnant mothers in Addis Ababa and orphan and disadvantaged girls.

The Sons Who Succeeded in Upholding the Covenant: Moa and Beniam Family Tradition of High Achievement

Moa and his wife Bethel   Beniam and his wife Li Jie

Moa and Beniam, the couple's two kids, are a blessing to Dr. Tesfaye and Mrs. Tersit. They take pride in the significant fraction they played in their adored boys' accomplishments.

Moa and Beniam have both completed their higher education. Additionally, they were actively involved in extracurricular activities. They both play musical instruments. In his fifth and eighth grade years, Beniam received the directors' award for playing the violin.

They had racial issues at school since they were black American pupils. According to Tesfaye,

"My wife and I have been mentoring them mostly on how they should face such racial problems at school, starting from their early youth. We frequently reminded them that they needed to work twice as hard to stand out from the crowd."

Fortunately, they both put in a lot of effort and had good time management skills. They've also succeeded professionally, which is a blessing for which we are grateful, says Tesfaye.

The most amazing blessings Mrs. Tersit has received from God are her two boys, Moa and Beniam. Using the values she had learned from her parents, she dedicated all of her time and energy to raising her sons. Dr Tesfaye has a son, Michael Biftu, from a previous relationship.

Moa, now 38 and employed by a significant health insurance provider, holds a Pharm.D. from the prestigious University of North Carolina Pharmacy School in Chapel Hill. Beniam, 37 years old, graduated from Rutgers University with a doctor of jurisprudence (JD) and an advanced law degree (LLM) from Georgetown Law Center.

"I have more pride in my boys' personalities and accomplishments—Beniam and Moa—than I do in my 100 patents; this pride is far more satisfying than any riches or income I could ever create in the US and Ethiopia.

Even though my contribution was less than my wife's, I am happy with my boys' successes. To me, my family comes before anything else. Love is the cornerstone of my family. Our relationship is quite close."

Dr. Tesfaye Biftu states,

"My family comes first above anything else in my life. Everything I achieve goes to my family - my wife, Tersit, and my two children, Moa and Beniam. The priceless time I spend with my family is the foundation of every joyful experience in my life."

Mrs. Tersit says the same to describe how much her devoted husband had contributed to their boys' outstanding accomplishments. She says,

"He loves his children very much. For the benefit of his children's lives, he has made sacrifices. He has established a close-knit friendship with

himself and his boys. He effectively put his own father's advice to use. He has made a significant contribution to his kids' successes."

Tesfaye and Tersit with Granddaughters Moriah, Gelila and Grandson Kaleb (Moa) Biftu

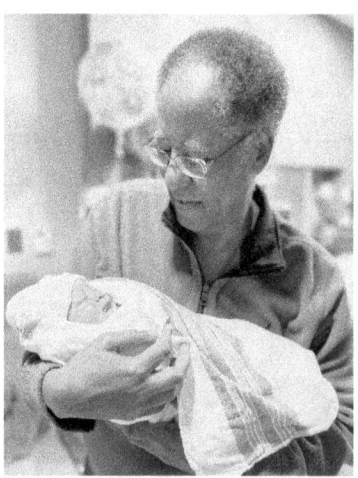

Tesfaye with Grandson Daniel (Beniam) Biftu

Chapter 10: Retirement Life

In 2016, Dr. Tesfaye Biftu departed Merck. He wrote the following letter to his coworkers:

Dear Friends and Colleagues,

I am leaving Merck after 35 years and 2 weeks of service. I joined the company as the first Senior African-American Chemist in Rahway when John Horan was the CEO in 1981. I came to the US as a student after completing high school in Ethiopia and a brief stay in France soon after the civil rights movement, and I am now leaving Merck at a historical time: President Barack Obama is the first African-American president of the USA, and Mr. Ken Frazier is the first African-American CEO of Merck!

Over the last 35 years, I was lucky to work with several talented colleagues, submit 12 clinical MK-candidates and key compounds, and over 120 patents and publications. Our selective DPP-8 compound has helped spur Januvia™ ahead of Novartis Galvus™, which at the time was five years ahead of us. Our latest discovery, the once weekly Marizev™, was approved in Japan a year ago in September 2015.

Our animal health candidate 411 is also progressing well in Germany. All of these are possible due to the support and excellent teamwork when I was given the opportunity to lead the DPP-4 and Animal Health Chemistry teams for several years. I like to thank you all for your hard work, creativity, and friendship. It is a privilege to have you as friends and colleagues. We are expecting a grandchild in December, and soon after that, I am looking forward to continuing my career in 2017.

I don't feel I am ready to retire yet!

Regards,
Tesfaye Biftu

Dr. Tesfaye received several replies, including a note from the Chairman of Merck, Ken Frazier, and the Research President Roger Perlmutter.

Dear Tes,

I wanted to offer my congratulations on your extraordinary career. Reflecting on the remarkable impact that you personally – through the supervision of chemical synthesis – have had on human and animal health during the past 35 years, you should feel enormously proud of your accomplishments.

Thank you for your leadership and dedication. You have made a real difference in the world. And for the future, I wish you fair winds and following seas. It has been a great adventure!

All best, RMP (Perlmutter, Roger M)
President of Merck Research labs

Following his departure from Merck, Dr. Tesfaye Biftu accepted a position as Distinguished Professor and Director of the Institute at Adama, Ethiopia's Institute of Pharmaceutical Sciences (IPS).

He also started lecturing at Addis Ababa University's Nutrition Department, where he had previously worked as an assistant professor before joining Merck in 1981.

Dr. Tesfaye also took on the role of Ph.D. mentor for Food and Nutrition as Medicine for Chronic Diseases.

He kept working as a Scientific Advisory Member for the Geneva-based Medicine for Malaria Venture (MMV).

Chapter 11: Community and Business Engagement

Dr. Tesfaye has participated extensively at various levels in a range of business and community activities. His exemplary effort in developing a powerful investment organization, particularly in the state of New Jersey, where he has resided with his family for decades. He has won the respect of friends and coworkers for his effort to strengthen the sense of community among Ethiopian Americans.

According to Ato Tekalign Gedamu, a project manager with Tesfaye,

"Besides being innovative and tenacious in pursuing goals, Tesfaye is continually inspired by a desire to engage in initiatives or ideas that assist his compatriots and immediate neighborhood. His range of academic interests is impressive. Tesfaye maintains his modesty despite having accomplished a lot."

The following list highlights some of Tesfaye Biftu's most significant professional and civic involvements.

Idir and Community Programs

Dr. Tesfaye has actively participated in social activities. He was the co-founder of one of the oldest Ethiopian-American Community organizations in Massachusetts, The Boston Ethiopian Community Organization, in 1981.

He is a member of IDIR, a 25-year-old self-help group for Ethiopians living in Delaware, Pennsylvania, and New Jersey. Additionally, he played a crucial part in the establishment of the Ethiopian-American Investment Group in 2013. Ato Tekalign Gedamu, described him as easygoing, constantly smiling, and having an unexpected sense of humor.

Tesfaye and his wife, Mrs. Tersit, made a concerted effort to raise their children with Ethiopian values.

This has been made possible in part through community organizations (Idir) but also in part by their steadfast efforts to educate them about Ethiopia's history, culture, and past background.

To prevent detachment and promote engagement with family members and other citizens, parents were keenly aware of the importance of instilling in their children a sufficient understanding of Ethiopia's past. This was one of the main drivers for the founding of the Idir. The children of Idir members attend regular meetings.

Children learn about cultural themes and artifacts during each gathering, including Ethiopian holidays, tales, characters, etc. Since its founding 25 years ago, Idir has been carrying out such activities. It has an important role in providing the kids with coaching and mentorship.

Tesfaye believes that the Idir has established a strong bond between its members and their children. Young people, teenagers, and even young boys and girls have benefited from the mentorship services offered by the Idir. Many of them now work as professionals, such as doctors, attorneys, accountants, engineers, social workers, and others who possess PhDs from US institutions.

Members of Idir represent many segments of Ethiopian society. In all of the Idir's history, ethnicity has never been a problem. Moreover, diversity has been very advantageous to the kids.

Dr. Tesfaye put together a book detailing the Idir's history and providing brief biographies of each member was released recently.

The photographs in the book feature children and portray them at various stages of growth.

Ethiopian Business and Industry Review (BIR)

Soon after the Derg dictatorship was toppled in the early 1990s, Tesfaye started and served as editor of the monthly publication known as **The Ethiopian Business and Industry Review.**

The goal was to offer a wide range of business, cultural, scientific, and technological information.

Tesfaye managed to publish the magazine each month despite working full-time at his regular job. Articles were submitted by well-known Ethiopian academics from many disciplines and artists.

Tesfaye describes how the publication first came to be:

"When I learned that Ethiopian publications issued at this time were solely political magazines, I got the idea to launch BIR. Personally, I thought there should be a separate publication that would focus on other significant subjects, such as economics, business, culture, science, and technology.

When BIR was founded, Ethiopia's military administration had just been deposed, and both domestic and international Ethiopians were heavily involved in political dialogue. I decided to launch a magazine that would concentrate on other equally significant themes after consulting with a few friends and academics."

Tesfaye said, "Unfortunately, there were two issues that made it impossible to continue the magazine's publishing. The dominance of political concerns increased and sustained, and BIR was unable to draw a large readership to support its continuous publication. Second, the firm I was working for (Merck) dramatically increased my positions and responsibilities. I didn't have much free time to complete the magazine publishing work. However, I intend to bring it once more in the future."

Tesfaye promoted community education in the State of New Jersey during his brief free time.

The Community Education Center has been in operation since 1994 and provides the general public with a wide range of courses on interesting and useful topics.

Tesfaye has frequently offered to volunteer to give seminars and to share his expertise about many facets of Ethiopia as part of this endeavor.

The Community Center coordinator praised Tesfaye Biftu's effort to provide seminars and stated,

"Your presentation was wonderful. Not only did you provide us with information on Ethiopian culture—facts, numbers, and fresh perspectives—but you also convinced us that we really need to keep learning more about it. Your teachings have led me to believe that Ethiopia is the eighth continent in the globe, even though it is still a part of Africa."

Ethiopian-American Investment Group

First team leaders to establish the first Ethiopian Community Bank in the USA
Standing left to right: Ato Bogale, Dr. Kitaw, Dr. Aberra, Ato Amha, Dr. Beniam
Sitting left to right: Dr. Tesfaye, Ato Tekalign, Dr. Melaku, Ato Cheru

Tesfaye Biftu has been collaborating with close friends since 1994 to establish an Ethiopian-American Community Bank. He initially started the project with one of his close friends, Mr. Fasil Gebremariam, who was senior vice-president of Florida General Telephone and Electricity. They recruited Mr. Tadesse Gebrekidan, a former Ethiopian governor, to do a market analysis. According to the analysis, the market was sufficiently large for the proposed bank.

Sadly, the project was never completed. The effort was launched not long after the Derg dictatorship was abolished. Politically, the neighborhood was severely polarized, making it very challenging to establish the bank.

Tesfaye and other businesses and professionals from Ethiopia never lost their goals. As a result, Tesfaye rekindled the concept of starting the bank among friends in Pennsylvania and New Jersey in 2012. Following a series of discussions between the professionals and businesspeople, the group came to the conclusion that it would be better to establish a company with the aim of investing in different enterprises delivering decent rates of return both in the US and Africa.

So, in December 2013, they established the "Ethiopian-American Investment Group (EAIG)." Now that the project's sustainability is established, Tesfaye is optimistic that his shared dream of founding a community bank will soon come to pass.

Tesfaye says, "We are progressing." I'm hoping Ethiopian Americans will soon have a local bank that will change the lives of many modest yet dedicated businesspeople," including Ato Tekalign Gedamu, chairman of EAIG, describes how Tesfaye has worked tirelessly to accomplish his shared goal as follows:

"When I arrived in the US, we met at a dinner party at a friend's house. During the meal, Tesfaye brought up a project that, in his opinion, might have a huge positive impact on the Ethiopian community in the U.S. Additionally, it could unite them and foster a favorable perception of the community abroad."

Tesfaye informed Ato Tekalign Gedamu that he was considering him as a potential project initiator who may play a significant part. He declared that he would do whatever it took to help the cause.

Ato Tekalign, who had been retired for more than ten years, responded that he didn't believe he had the stamina to take on the part Tesfaye had in mind for him.

Tesfaye made a second request a few weeks later because he was still not persuaded. In spite of the fact that the concept was a great one, Ato Tekalign attempted to explain why he wasn't the best choice for the job being considered. Tesfaye, however, did not let go. This continued for several months. Tesfaye's tenacious insistence forced Ato Tekalign to give in in the end.

A group of 70 well-known figures joined hands and initiated the project.

Chapter 12: International Recognition, Honors, and Achievements

Due to his exceptional contributions to the discovery of medications, Dr. Tesfaye has won several worldwide accolades, recognitions, and awards as a top medical scientist.

Here are some of the most recognized achievements of Dr. Tesfaye.

Position among International Who's Who of Professionals

The above speakers at the Lisbon, Portugal conference were Sabine Hadida (Vertex Pharmaceuticals) who reported on Ivacaftor, an approved drug for the treatment of cystic fibrosis; Tesfaye Biftu (Merck), the inventor of Omarigliptin, a new therapy for type II diabetes; Henning Steinhagen (Grunhental), the inventor of Cebepranodolm a new therapy for cancer pain in phase II of clinical trials; Georg Jaeschke (Roche), the inventor of Basimglurant, a novel therapy for the treatment-resistant depression in phase II of clinical trials and Ada Yonath (Weizmann Institute of Sciences, Israel, and Nobel Laureate 2009) who gave her personal vision on the importance of basic research for the invention of new medicines

Dr. Tesfaye is a remarkable scientist whose name appeared in the 1998 edition of the **"International Who's Who of Professionals"** publication, which profiles higher achievers in America.

This American series features individuals' accomplishments in major spheres of public or professional life and pays tribute to the exceptional achievements of American professionals.

Only this special edition will honor those people in the United States who are destined to significantly impact both American and global society in the future.

After undertaking a series of thorough evaluations, **International Who's Who of Professionals** selected Dr. Tesfaye from a pool of contenders to receive its accolade on January 29, 1998.

*"We want to give you a certificate of achievement and a press release announcing in the **International Who's Who of Professionals** 1998 edition. The certificate serves as a standout memento of your accomplishments. Your name will be highlighted in calligraphy, announcing your inclusion in the elite group of successful people."*

The announcement was that a world-class Afro-American scientist named Dr. Tesfaye Biftu had been included in the **Worldwide Who's Who of Professionals.**

Outstanding Scientist and Model

SEED Award 1996: Dr. Getachew Haile and Dr. Tesfaye Biftu

Dr. Tesfaye Biftu was chosen as a renowned scientist and an inspiration to fellow diaspora Ethiopians, African-Americans, and others on May 26, 1996, by the **Society of Ethiopians Established in Diaspora** (SEED) and the Ethiopian Pharmacists and Pharmaceutical Association Scientists in Diaspora (2021).

A non-profit organization called **SEED** was founded to safeguard the rights of Ethiopians living abroad and the interests of their offspring, as well as to promote their active participation in community activities.

One of Tesfaye Biftu's collegues, Dr. Thomas N. Salzmann, Senior Vice President at Merck and Co. confirmed the **SEED**'s selection of Tesfaye Biftu by writing to SEED and expressing his congratulations.

"You certainly could not have chosen better, in my opinion. Tesfaye and I have been friends for over 15 years. I've had a lot of respect for him as a scientist and a man throughout that period. Tesfaye has engaged in several endeavors outside of science just in the last

few years, as I have come to learn. It is quite amazing what Tes has accomplished, and it speaks volumes about his dedication, vigor, and sense of duty that permeate everything he does. Tes has been able to make such significant contributions to his country while also upholding the greatest standards of scientific brilliance. I consider myself extremely blessed to have Tes as both a friend and a coworker. His capacity to elevate individuals around him makes him a unique type of person."

Thus, SEED celebrated Dr. Tesfaye's outstanding accomplishment on May 26, 1996, in Washington, D.C., in the presence of well-known and esteemed dignitaries from many spheres of society.

SEED stated on Tesfaye's letter of selection:

"You are, in every way, worthy of the distinction. We are pleased with the acknowledgement that SEED has given you. Your selection for this honorary title is an encouraging example of how well you are regarded."

Award for 1993's Best Scientist - CytoMed

During his two years as Head of Chemistry at CytoMed, Dr. Tesfaye set an example of the highest level of scientific leadership (1993-1994). As a result, CytoMed honored him with the **"Scientist of the Year 1993"** award in recognition of his remarkable accomplishment.

The organization commended Tesfaye's exceptional scientific leadership and accomplishments in bestowing him with the special prize. According to a statement, Dr. Tesfaye, the winner of the **"Scientist of the Year"** award, was honored largely for his scientific leadership and inventiveness. Furthermore, CytoMed praised how Dr. Tesfaye Biftu's talents have positively affected all of the company's initiatives, especially the Epibatidine and DFA programs.

His efforts have been priceless in and of themselves, but he has also motivated us at CytoMed to strive for the same standard of perfection. His wisdom and sense of teamwork have spurred a high level of dedication and output, the company confirmed.

Furthermore, as the company's leaders themselves would attest, Tesfaye's scientific leadership helped the organization become competent and successful in the years that followed. They said: *"The qualities established by Tesfaye are what we should all strive for in ourselves and what will continue to make CytoMed successful."*

Honorable Judge for Scientific Fairs

For his significant contribution as a judge in science, art, and technology fairs held in his state of New Jersey, Dr. Tesfaye was recognized by several commissions.

One such commission that has been holding similar fairs on science, art, and technology, and where Dr. Tesfaye sat as a judge on the Martin Luther King Commemorative Commission.

Martin Luther King Commemorative Commission wrote to Dr. Tesfaye in appreciation of the fair and honest evaluation he provided during one of these science fair competitions:

"Without a doubt, the success of the day was directly related to the encouragement, motivation, and careful consideration you gave to each contestant. Above all, you displayed a keen sense of fairness and resolve to judge on a relative, not absolute, basis" the Commission commended Tesfaye in the letter of honor delivered to him.

Part II: VIEWS AND OPINIONS

Chapter 13: Observations on the Political and Historical Systems of Ethiopia

Modern Ethiopian history and Emperor Haile Selassie I

Dr. Tesfaye's analysis of Ethiopian political structures and regimes is based on his observations and personal knowledge, free from ideological or racial connotations. Tesfaye holds Emperor Haile Selassie in high regard since he started Ethiopia's transition to a modern nation-state and established significant public institutions.

He has strong arguments supporting his stance on Emperor Haile Selassie that are both compelling and practical. Although he controlled the nation as a kind of despot, Emperor Haile Selassie was successful in his modernization program.

The Emperor's effectiveness supports Dr. Tesfaye's assessment of establishing contemporary structures and organizations to benefit the nation. He spent a significant portion of his life in Ethiopia under the rule of Emperor Haile Selassie and can attest firsthand to the achievements of the Emperor for his nation.

"When I was 18 years old, I had three personal encounters with Emperor Haile Selassie. I initially met him when he brought Queen

Elizabeth II to visit my school in 1963, then I met him again on the day I received my degree from Bahir Dar Polytechnic School. Later, at the Hawassa Oil facility, when he came to manage the business I was then in charge of, I ran into him again. In this sense, I'm fortunate. But it's not because I've met him three times that he has my adoration; it's because of the revolutionary changes he brought about in Ethiopia."

Tesfaye holds a good impression of Emperor Haile Selassie because of the reforms he made to the nation, which, in his opinion, served as the foundation for creating a modern Ethiopian state.

Ethiopia was an unenlightened, somewhat disjointed nation when the Emperor came to power. The Emperor employed a variety of tactics to promote national harmony.

Tesfaye asserts, *"I do not analyze the government from the perspective of modern and evolved political systems. Of course, the Emperor governed medieval Ethiopia as an absolute monarchy like his predecessors. But I think the Emperor's nation-building initiatives were primarily responsible for Ethiopia reaching its current status.*

Through subtle and overt political actions, the Emperor has contributed significantly to developing a strong feeling of Ethiopian nationality.

He purposefully planned, for instance, that his children and grandkids marry into several ethnic groups outside of the Shoah, Amhara, Oromo, and Tigre. Tesfaye says he also elevated people from many ethnic and religious groups to high political and military posts.

Public Institutions Established During Emperor Haile Selassie's Reign and Their Importance to Modern-Day Ethiopia

Another quality Tesfaye admires in Haile Selassie is the establishment of many international and regional organizations as part of his modernization drive.

He said,

"At the national level, Emperor Haile Selassie's administration launched the majority of Ethiopia's contemporary institutions and public services. For instance, during his rule, modern schooling was made available in more sections of the country; telecommunications, postal, and road services were also introduced. The Ethiopian Airlines and Commercial Bank of Ethiopia are two examples of the enormous government-run businesses that the Emperor founded. I think the Emperor was responsible for establishing Ethiopia's contemporary public institutions, too. Additionally, the Emperor was committed to advancing the values of world peace and security and creating Pan-African organizations."

A consolidated legal system was established under Emperor Haile Selassie. He set up a modern financial system and centralized taxation to raise his nation to international standards.

He also established the Ethiopian Telecommunications Authority and Ethiopian Airlines to connect the nation with the outside world. His vision has yielded many educated Ethiopians today and the first stages of the nation's infrastructure. The following sections provide an overview of the evolution in history and the importance of some of the public institutions established by Emperor Haile Selassie in modern-day Ethiopia.

The purpose of highlighting the histories and profiles of the public institutions is to demonstrate Emperor Haile Selassie's significant contributions to establishing the modern Ethiopian state.

Commercial Bank of Ethiopia and State Bank

After the Ethiopian English victory against Fascist Italy in August 1942, the administration of Emperor Haile Selassie issued a decree creating the State Bank of Ethiopia. On April 15, 1943, the State Bank of Ethiopia officially opened its doors with two branches and 43 employees. It operated as the primary commercial bank in Ethiopia and the central bank, which had the authority to print money on behalf of the ministry of finance.

In 1945, the Imperial government gave the bank exclusive authority to issue money. George Blowers, an American, served as the bank's first governor. He introduced the new national currency, whose practical introduction was made possible by American support.

In 1980, the Ethiopian government merged Addis Bank into the Commercial Bank of Ethiopia (CBE), becoming CBE the only commercial bank in the nation. It was done in response to the nationalization of private banks and corporate entities following the 1974 revolution. The private Addis Ababa Bank and the privately held Banco di Roma and Banco di Napoli's Ethiopian businesses came together to become Addis Bank. There were 26 branches of Addis Ababa Bank at the time of nationalization. With 128 units and 3,633 staff, CBE was the only Ethiopia's commercial bank following the merger of Addis Ababa Bank and CBE until new banks were allowed to open in again after 1992.

The current Ethiopian government reformed and restarted CBE in 1994. Ethiopia's most prominent commercial bank is the Commercial Bank of Ethiopia (CBE). Its assets were at 22 billion US$ as of October 2022, and it controlled over 67% of the nation's bank deposits and 53% of all bank loans.

The bank employs over 22,000 people in its headquarters and over 900 branches throughout major cities and small villages, including 120 locations in Addis Ababa, the country's capital.

Ethiopian Airlines (EAL)

Emperor Haile Selassie created Ethiopian Airlines on December 21, 1945. It has since grown to be one of the fastest-growing businesses in its sector and one of the biggest on the African continent. The Emperor established the airline with an initial investment of ETB 2.5 million split into 25,000 shares wholly controlled by the government.

The Ethiopian government provided funding, while TWA, an American enterprise, operated the business. Beginning with its General Managers, it was reliant on American pilots, technicians, administrators, and accountants.

Fitawrari Tafasse Habte Mikael, Minister of Work and Communications, was named the first president and chairman of Ethiopian Airlines. At the same time, American H. H. Holloway was chosen by TWA to serve as General Manager.

On April 8, 1946, Ethiopian Airlines launched its first regularly scheduled commercial flight on the Addis Ababa-Asmara-Cairo route with one of five Douglas C-47 Skytrains it had purchased from the U.S. government. Later, this service began operating once a week.

Soon after, the airline began flying to Aden and Djibouti, as well as a local trip to Jimma. Addis Ababa-Asmara, Addis Ababa-Djibouti-Aden,

Addis Ababa-Khartoum, Addis Ababa-Cairo (via Jeddah or Khartoum), and Asmara-Khartoum were the major five routes.

Alemayehu Abebe, the first Ethiopian to command a commercial aircraft, completed his first solo flight in a DC-3/C-47.

Ethiopian Airlines successfully secured aircraft as part of its strategic business plan throughout the 1960s and 1970s while the Emperor was still in the country. On July 15, 1960, a DC-3 traveling from Bulchi to Jimma crashed, killing the pilot and inflicting the first fatal accident for the airline.

Ethiopian Air Lines became Ethiopian Airlines after the airline's legal status changed from corporation to share company in 1965. The sixth renewal of the original 1945 contract upgraded TWA's position from Manager to Adviser in 1970. The business was prepared to run without outside help in 1971 when it celebrated its 25th anniversary.

Since that time, Ethiopians have been in charge of running and staffing Ethiopian Airlines. Col. Semret Medhane was chosen as the first general manager of Ethiopia and was appointed in 1971.

The airlines initially saw a fall in service quality and revenues after the revolution of 1974 and the Dreg's interference in their administration. Later, though, it permitted the airline to operate on a "strictly commercial basis." Despite the Soviet Union and the communist government's cooperation, the airline kept buying Western rather than Soviet-made aircraft, buying Boeing 727 in 1979 and Boeing 767 in 1984. Ethiopian was the first airline in Africa to buy the Boeing 767 and Boeing 767-200ER in 1982.

Additionally, Ethiopia received the first of five Boeing 757-200s in 1991, making it the first passenger airline to receive the Boeing 757

Freighter. After the EPRDF took office in 1996, the airline began operating flights to Bangkok, Beijing, Durban, and Johannesburg. It also had links to the Ivory Coast and Senegal. The airline joined the Star Alliance in December 2011, becoming the 28th member overall and the third African airline to do so (after Egypt Air and South African Airways).

Ethiopian Airlines now offers service to 23 cargo destinations, 19 domestic, and 114 passenger international destinations. Ethiopians serve more African cities than any other airline.

It is one of the fastest-growing businesses in the sector and one of the biggest on the continent of Africa. Additionally, it is one of the few successful airlines operating in the sub-Saharan region. At the 41st Annual Airline Industry Achievement Awards presented by Air Transport World (ATW) on February 25, 2015, in Washington, D.C., Ethiopia recently took home the trophy for Best Regional Airline of the Year. In 2012, the carrier reported a BIRR 2.031 billion yearly profit and employed around 8,066 people.

Telecommunications in Ethiopia

Emperor Haile Selassie first founded Ethiopian Telecommunications Corporation (ETC) under the Imperial Board of Telecommunications of Ethiopia (IBTE) by proclamation No. 131/52 in 1952. ETC was later renamed Ethio Telecom.

The corporation operated independently from the Ministry of Posts, Telephones, and Telegraphs. During the Imperial era, the corporation set the path for the country's economic growth. The Derg administration reformed the IBTE in October 1975 to become the Ethiopian Telecommunications Service and again in January 1981 to become the Ethiopian Telecommunications Authority.

The Ethiopian Telecommunications Authority changed its name to Ethiopian Telecommunications (ETC) in November 1996 due to the Council of Ministers Regulation No. 10/1996. Proclamation No. 49/1996 later increased ETC's obligations.

In Ethiopia, Ethio Telecom, formerly the Ethiopian Telecommunications Corporation (ETC), is a supplier of integrated telecommunications services that offers internet and telephone services. The Ethiopian government owns Ethio Telecom, which controls all telecommunications services in Ethiopia.

It is one of Ethiopia's "Big-5" groupings of state-owned businesses, together with Ethiopian Airlines, the Commercial Bank of Ethiopia, Ethio-Insurance, and the Ethiopian Shipping Lines. It has headquarters in Addis Ababa.

Ethiopian Post

Before the Italian invasion of Ethiopia in 1936, the administration of Emperor Haile Selassie opened the General Post Office and two branch offices in Addis Ababa.

Additionally, 36 new post offices were established around the empire. Following the Italian fascist invasion, the growth of postal services was halted. Except for the ones in Harar, Dire Dawa, and Addis Ababa, the occupying forces demolished all of the offices in the areas. They have tried to restructure the Ethiopian Postal Service to suit their requirements.

According to the post office's official website history, everything had to be rebuilt when the Italian fascist troops were routed, and Ethiopian independence was restored in 1941. Emperor Haile Selassie founded the Ministry of Posts, Telegraphs, and Telephones to hasten the restoration of the nation's war-devastated communications infrastructure.

The post office was given autonomy and a Director General to oversee it throughout the reign of the Emperor. In turn, the Director General carried out his responsibilities while supervised by a Minister. The Addis Ababa postal headquarters oversaw the general management and financial operations of the post service.

The Postal Services Division at the Headquarters coordinated and oversaw the 12 postal districts, each led by a Head Postmaster. When the General Post Office building was built in 1969, it had enough room to accommodate the expansion of postal services in new locations.

The postal museum was constructed seven years after the general post office.

Ethiopia now has over 1139 post offices, covering an area of 1.1 million km2 and a population of 110 million. In addition to 2 visiting mail carriers in rural regions and more than 170,000 post boxes, there are 746 permanent post offices, 130 departmental sub-post offices, and 261 sub-post offices. A private box is considered to serve 529 persons, whereas a post office serves 79,016 residents.

In 1989, the Ethiopian Postal Service launched EMS (express mail service). The implementation of EMS has increased the service's competitiveness in the express delivery industry.

Encouragement of International Collective Security

Emperor Haile Selassie became a worldwide celebrity overnight because of his famous speech to the League of Nations on June 30, 1936, in which he called for a collective response to Italy's invasion of his land. He was no longer merely the inconspicuous monarch of a little-known northeast African kingdom.

Instead, over the 1920s, 1930s, and 1940s, he rose to prominence as a global leader and a well-known representative of the fascist regime that had its origins in Italy and had now extended to other central European countries.

Pan-Africanism and the Organization of African Unity

According to Dr. Tesfaye, one of the most important events he has seen in his life is the founding of the Organization of African Unity (OAU). The establishment of the A.U. has given Africans, in general, and Ethiopia, in particular, an organizational framework to advance in the direction of development.

Indeed, bringing together two opposing political factions to form "an organization that would unify all of Africa" was one of Emperor Haile Selassie's most outstanding achievements—and there were many.

In 1963, 32 members of the OAU designated HIM as the "Father of African Unity" in commemoration of this outstanding accomplishment.

The Organization of African Unity (OAU) was founded on May 25, 1963, and has its permanent headquarters in Addis Ababa, Ethiopia. Emperor of Ethiopia Haile Selassie was chosen as the OAU's first chairman. Emperor Haile Selassie said the following in his acceptance address before the leaders of the 32 member nations:

"Today is a historic and historic day for Africa and all Africans. The audience of global opinion is watching us from the stage of international

politics today. We have gathered to demonstrate our influence over global affairs and fulfill our responsibility to the enormous continent we are in charge of, home to 250 million people.

Africa is currently in the middle of its evolution, moving from the Africa of the past to the Africa of the future. Even as we stand here, we move into the future from the past. The mission of "creating Africa" that we have undertaken will not be delayed. We must take action to mold the future and leave our imprint on the events as they pass into history."

Before the OAU was founded, African nations were divided into several opposing groupings: English- and French-speaking, progressive (the Casablanca group), and moderate (the Monrovia group). The Casablanca group demanded an immediate unity government for all of Africa. On the other hand, the Monrovian bloc believed that unity should be accomplished gradually through economic cooperation.

The idea of instantaneous unity was not supported. Fascinatingly, the conflict was finally settled when Ethiopian Emperor Haile Selassie cordially welcomed the two factions to Addis Ababa and convinced them to establish OAU. It didn't seem possible at first. However, the Emperor persevered and was successful in bringing everyone on board.

Addis Ababa was chosen as the organization's base of operations, and a charter was signed.

The OAU was restructured in July 2002 under African Unity (A.U.). The European Union (E.U.) appeared to be a promising model, with 54 members. The goal of the Union was to expand on the work of the OAU by creating a body that might hasten the integration of Africa, encourage African governments' involvement in the global economy, and handle the complex social, economic, and political issues that the continent faces.

Kofi Annan, a Ghanaian and former U.N. Secretary-General, praised the organization for bringing Africans together. However, some contend that in its 39 years of existence, the OAU accomplished nothing to protect African citizens' rights and liberties from their political leaders. They refer to it as the "Dictators' Club" or the "Dictator's Trade Union."

The OAU was effective in specific ways. Many of its members were also U.N. members, banding together to protect African interests, particularly in light of still-existing colonialism. However, its efforts to solidify and integrate the African economy fell short. A resurrected organization in the form of A.U. felt appropriate. So, a decision was made.

In May 2013, historians and former political figures met in Addis Ababa to commemorate the 50th anniversary of the Organization of African Unity (OAU) and Emperor Haile Selassie's role in its formation. Thabo Mbeki, a former president of South Africa who served on the panel, praised Haile Selassie's contribution to the founding of the OAU and the battle for African independence in his keynote speech.

"It is the responsibility of this generation to reflect on and extol the merits of the contributions made by past African leaders that helped to advance Africa to where it is now. Emperor Haile Selassie made significant contributions to the unity of African states and the liberation of Africa from colonialism."

Chapter 14: Opinions on Religion, Ethnic Politics, and Ethnicity in Ethiopia

Religion and Ethnicity in Ethiopia

Dr. Tesfaye claims that ethnic politics have been the main driver behind Ethiopia's development after the fall of the Derg dictatorship. Instead of coming from one or another abstract ideological standpoint, Dr. Tesfaye's perspective on ethnicity and ethnic politics is based on his personal experience.

According to Dr. Tesfaye, *"The majority of Ethiopians may not claim homogeneity in terms of Ethnic heritage." Consider, for instance, my background,"* he says.

"My father is Illu Abba Bor-born Oromo. In my opinion, my father's ancestors must have intermarried with inhabitants of the nearby communities.

The same is true for my mother, whose ancestors are from Wollo in northern Ethiopia's Amhara ethnic group. The ancestor of my mother must have intermarried with other people who lived in the north of Ethiopia, too. I would describe myself as an Oromo based on the Oromo culture of genealogy research, which exclusively considers the father's line. I cannot, however, state categorically or solely that I am an Oromo ethnic group member for these reasons."

According to Merera (2006), ethnic politics considerably impact modern Ethiopian political ideas, mobilizations, and organizations. However, there are divergent opinions on the contribution of ethnicity and ethnic politics to the development of Ethiopian polity.

He explains that three opposing viewpoints—the nation-building perspective, the national domination perspective, and the colonial thesis—have dominated Ethiopia's political structure.

The proponents of the nation-building approach claim that ethnicity is something that can be formed and reshaped rather than something pre-made. Ethnic identity is primarily shaped, created, and perpetuated by the state. They also contend that ethnicity is a social construct and not a unique aspect of national identity. The nation-building viewpoint adherent Solomon Teshale makes this argument in his series of research publications titled **"Nationalism and Ethnic Conflict in Ethiopia."**

He also makes a compelling case that recognizing the Amhara-Tigre core culture's hegemonic dominance was necessary for Ethiopia to become a sovereign nation, resulting in the assimilation of other identities into the Amhara language, culture, religion, etc. He believes that the Amhara people's fundamental culture supports other ethnic groups in feeling a sense of national identity.

On the other hand, the proponents of the ethno-nationalist position would contend that Ethiopians from the north, south, east, and west have different cultures, languages, and religions.

Herbert Lewis, an advocate of the ethnonational view on Ethiopian politics and author of several books, would contend that all conquered people had separate identities before being ruled by Ethiopian rulers.

Lewis also believed that the presence of more than 70 languages in Ethiopia strongly indicates different identities among Ethiopia's ethnic groupings. Furthermore, he said that individuals in the north and the south had been engaging in completely distinct political ideologies, ranging from monarchical to egalitarianism in the south, particularly among the Oromo.

"I usually want to identify myself as an Ethiopian," Dr. Tesfaye says when discussing ethnicity in Ethiopia.

"But I never approve of ethnic hierarchies or disparities in Ethiopia or Ethiopian politics. As a natural scientist, I am quite aware that although people can be divided into different races depending on where they live, they all sprang from the same biological origin."

Dr. Tesfaye further argues,

"Obviously, humans exist on all continents. There are various ethnic groups coexisting on all continents. Ethiopia, with over 80 ethnic groupings, cannot be any different, in my opinion. An Ethiopian may be of Oromo, Amhara, Tigre, Somali, Afar, Gurage, or another ethnic or mixed group. The fact that all ethnic groups are members of the human race is, in reality, their primary point of commonality. Ethiopia cannot be an exception to this rule, obviously. While ethnic or racial variety has also significantly impacted how people communicate, being human may be more important than any other component in all relationships."

He also contends that for Ethiopia to improve in all areas of development and modernization, it is more important to emphasize commonalities between ethnic groups or nations than disparities between them. He claims that to guarantee the greatest level of wealth and growth that would benefit all Ethiopians, Ethiopians must put a strong emphasis on humanity.

Dr. Tesfaye maintains pragmatist and practical views regarding religion and its function in interpersonal relationships and other areas.

Again, his perspective is based on his real-world experience, which dates back to his early years in Agaro, where he was born.

"I grew up in Agaro, where the local populations practiced Christianity and Islam. So, despite coming from a Christian background, I guess I understood just as much about Islam as my Muslim friends did. As a result, I was raised as a "Chrislam," a Christian with a profound grasp of Islam.

The Byzantine/Roman, Persian, and Abyssinian empires were all around Arabia when Mohammad started reading verses from the Quran. I had acquaintances who practiced Islam, and because of the ancient tradition that went back many generations, religion never stood as a barrier separating us.

We stayed at each other's houses and were free to play and study together. The only thing that separated us was that neither of us went to church or the mosque together. Such practical experiences molded my perspective of religious equality and tolerance in my youth.

I finished my graduate studies at Brandeis University, founded by the Jewish community, even after moving to the US in 1971. I was also allowed to learn more about many global faiths because of this exposure," he says.

He hardly ever comprehended the distinctions and conflicts between many religions and religious institutions as a kid or even after moving to the US. As Ethiopia's two main religions recognize the reality of the Almighty God, he found the similarities between Islam and Christianity more logical than the differences.

"I didn't discover the factors behind religious disparities until I immigrated to the US and learned more interesting perspectives and views. Even though I am aware of the distinctions between faiths and religious organizations, I firmly think that religious diversity should never cause any argument or conflict.

My early life taught me that individuals of various religious beliefs might coexist peacefully, provided they know one another's beliefs and respect them. The primary precondition for people living in peace wherever in the world is the existence of respect and acceptance between followers of all religions. I choose to agree with one of Emperor Haile Selassie's famous quotes in this regard: "A country belongs to all, religion belongs to individuals."

Perspective on Ethiopian Regimes in the Past and Present

Tesfaye criticizes Ethiopia's past and present governments for their contributions to the country's growth on several fronts. He cites the Ethiopian administrations' failure to continue the advancements made by their forerunners as one of their main shortcomings.

Despite having different state structures, the three Ethiopian regimes—Emperor Haile Selassie, the Derg, and the EPRDF—seem to have several functional similarities. While the Derg was a left-wing dictatorship, Emperor Haile Selassie's government was a classic authoritarian monarchy. The current leadership, the EPRDF, has chosen an ethnic federal state structure.

Despite their differences, these regimes have annihilated the work of their predecessors, regardless of their strengths or detriments. For instance, the Derg started from scratch after destroying all of the Haile Selassie regime's work on Ethiopian Airlines. Similarly, the EPRDF government chose to make a fresh start by dismantling all institutions and regulations by the Derg dictatorship, regardless of their strengths or shortcomings.

Nobody can predict how this cycle will stop. In Dr. Tesfaye's opinion, it is one of Ethiopia's most significant obstacles to its political progress. Only a few nations in the world have managed to create a thriving government by obliterating the infrastructure that previous governments had built. Every regime has both positive and negative aspects.

The goal of succeeding administrations should be to build on the positive changes made while addressing the shortcomings of earlier ones. It is how developed nations were able to achieve their current status.

Dr. Biftu contends that something must be done to prevent the total loss of everything previous administrations had achieved if Ethiopia is to advance on the country's wealth and growth path.

The Ethiopian government's disinterest in a peaceful transfer of power, which is the norm in other African nations, is another flaw in their systems.

Tesfaye also points out that political leaders in Ethiopia want to maintain their positions of power indefinitely. Because they are worried about their safety and are aware that if they are removed from office, they would be held accountable for whatever wrongdoings they committed during their tenure.

According to Dr. Tesfaye, Ethiopia should implement the political changes that its people demand. It should include a democratic political system in which all citizens participate, exercising their right to free speech, freely choosing their leaders, and voluntarily contributing to their nation's economic and social development.

Chapter 15: Views on The US Political System

The Distinctive Characteristics of the US System

Dr. Tesfaye is an African American scientist who has spent more than 40 years living in the US. He knows that the US political system has several distinctive aspects that conflict with one another.

Dr. Tesfaye pointed out that the US political system has mainly always been characterized by two ideologically opposing concepts, making it more difficult politically than any other nation.

On one side, there is a significant racial difference in the nation, and as a result, race plays a vital role in the US political system. While, on the flip side, despite significant racial differences, there is a high level of national integrity and solidarity among the people. The nation's long-standing, distinctive political culture makes it easier to deal with these fundamental conflicts.

Instead, detractors would contend that race plays a significant role in American politics. The cornerstone of the American political system is systemic racial oppression, a result of past injustices ranging from the use of slavery to the Jim Crow laws.

A new racial gap has formed between the 'race-conscious' policies espoused by the liberals and the 'colorblind' policies of the conservatives, even though modern advancements have moved politics beyond historical racial conflicts.

The idea of a "colorblind" America initially seems appealing. But when given more thought, assertions that American politics are colorblind or post-racial negatively affect the institutionalized racial tensions and biases.

Colorblind policies not only obscure racial differences but also keep silent about present-day injustices and inequality. In the United States, racism is institutionalized due to more than three centuries of legislated racial discrimination.

Critics would also contend that although race is still integral to the US political system, black Americans have seen enormous strides ahead and the current racial impasse.

Half a century after the historic "I Have a Dream" freedom speech of Martin Luther King, in 1963, the renowned and experienced US journalist Steven A. Holmes reflected on the trends of US racial challenges:

"Since then, events and trends have shaped the civil rights struggle and today's racial landscape having the most impact over time on the well-being of blacks and whites and on their underlying attitudes toward each other."

Some of the directional markers are well-known, while others are less obvious. Some helped the country move toward racial peace, while others served as significant obstacles. Beyond racial differences, many have altered American culture. All of these shifted the course of racial history.

Dr. Tesfaye pointed out that the US system's paradoxes can also be seen in the stark differences between people's lives, periodically getting more expansive. But because the US is one of the nations where people have actual influential voices and freedom, he expects greed that drives enormous discrepancy between affluent and poor individuals will be reduced in the future by genuine citizen engagement.

The US system, above all, allows all citizens, regardless of origin, to work and develop themselves. For instance, the majority of immigrants were poor or lacking in resources. But today, with their hard work, immigrants from different ethnic groups live the same quality of living as any middle-class American.

Republicans and Democrats

The Democrats and the Republicans are the two main parties that currently dominate American politics. Despite considerable distinctions between Democrats and Republicans, it would be complicated to categorize everyone based on all political issues.

There are several significant areas in which members of each party agree. Understanding their core values, viewpoints, and how they have stayed true to them through their voting history is also essential.

The Federalist Party and its nationalist ideologies were fiercely opposed by Jefferson's Republicans, who had their origins in Thomas Jefferson. At that time, the Democratic Party was known as Jefferson's Republicans. In commemorating Andrew Jackson, dubbed "jackass" in public for advocating "let the people govern," the Democrats chose the donkey as their emblem.

In 1848, the Democratic National Committee was formally established. The party split during the Civil War between those who supported and opposed slavery. A new democratic party, the one we know today, was founded due to this severe rift.

On the other side, because of their long-standing support for the abolition of slavery, the Republican Party was founded soon before the Civil War. They were a tiny third party that put forth John C. Freemont's presidential nomination in 1856. When their candidate Abraham Lincoln was elected president of the United States in 1860, they established themselves as a legitimate political force.

Lincoln's leadership throughout the war, notably his initiatives to permanently abolish slavery, contributed to the Republican Party's emergence as a significant force in American politics. They decided on the elephant as its emblem in 1874 after seeing a caricature of the new party as an elephant in Harper's Weekly.

Ideological Differences Between The Democrats and Republicans

According to the literature, several fundamental distinctions emerged due to the development of a strong two-party system in the United States, with the Democrats starting in 1824 and the Republicans beginning in 1854. The political ideas that separate the two are pretty strong, and some of them are as follows:

Fiscal Policy

Both the democratic and republican parties support tax cuts, but they have differing ideas on how to implement them. Democrats think tax rates should be higher for companies and rich people and that cuts should only be made for middle-class and low-income households. Republicans, meanwhile, believe that tax rates should be reduced for everyone, including businesses and individuals with all income levels.

Social Problems

Democrats and Republicans have different perspectives on social problems, one of their main distinctions. On social matters, Republicans often have conservative views. For instance, they frequently advocate for heterosexual marriage while opposing homosexual marriage.

They support the freedom to bear arms and are against abortion. Democrats, on the other hand, tend to have more liberal viewpoints and support homosexual marriage and abortion, but they also vehemently advocate strict gun control regulations restricting ownership.

Employment and Free Trade

When it comes to the corporate sector, Democrats and Republicans hold quite different views. Republicans often oppose raising the minimum wage, arguing that businesses must keep prices low to thrive and provide goods and services to all Americans.

Democrats, meanwhile, support raising the minimum wage so that Americans might have more money to spend on things. Republicans promote free trade to keep costs low for consumers and increase company profitability so they may expand, while Democrats support trade restrictions to safeguard American employment.

Health Care

Democrats often support extensive government control over the health care system, including the enactment of the Affordable Care Act, because it makes the system widely accessible. Republicans, who fought against the Affordable Treatment Act, think that excessive government intervention in the healthcare sector would increase expenses and negatively affect the standard of care that patients get.

Social Initiatives

All Democrats agree that the government should manage social welfare programs like Medicaid, food stamps, poverty, and unemployment compensation for those in need. They think that more tax money needs to be allocated to these initiatives.

Republicans agree that these social services are necessary but want to cut the budget and tighten oversight. Republicans like to support businesses that help those in need.

Foreign Affairs

Foreign policy is a significant point of contention between Democrats and Republicans. Over the years, each party has taken different positions on foreign policy based on the circumstances. Republicans want a comprehensive military effort to topple totalitarian governments that harm their people and threaten others.

At the same time, Democrats generally advocate more targeted strikes and sparing use of troops when military action may be necessary. Typically, all parties concur that providing help to other nations is worthwhile, but they dispute the kind of aid to offer and who should get it.

Climate Change and Energy Issues

Conflicts between the parties over environmental and energy-related concerns have long existed. Republicans support expanding drilling to create more energy at a reduced cost to customers, while Democrats support banning drilling for oil or other fossil fuels to safeguard the environment. Democrats will promote and fund the development of alternative energy sources with tax monies, in contrast to Republicans, who prefer letting the market choose which energy sources are practicable.

Education

The parties disagree on several aspects of the nation's educational system, but they all agree that something has to change. While Republicans tend to advocate more conservative measures like longer hours and more specialized programs, Democrats tend to favor more progressive approaches to education, such as establishing the Common Core System.

Additionally, there is disagreement regarding college student loans, with Democrats preferring increased funding for students in the form of grants and loans. At the same time, Republicans advocate encouraging the private sector to provide loans rather than the government.

Crime and the Death Penalty

Republicans typically support more severe punishments for crimes like drug sales. Additionally, they keep a system with multiple levels to guarantee that exemplary punishment has been applied and typically support the death penalty.

Democrats hold progressive ideas and think nonviolent offenses like drug sales should have lenient punishments and rehabilitation. They oppose all forms of the death penalty.

Individual Liberty

Individual liberty has recently been a hot topic. Many think people need to be safeguarded from themselves since political correctness is on the rise. Democrats have a history of supporting legislation that limits our liberties, including our access to certain foods. Republicans support individual freedom, believing that, as long as it doesn't violate the law, people should be free to decide for themselves what they do and don't do.

The United States Under the Obama Administration

Dr. Tesfaye is a fervent supporter of the Democratic Party, one of the two modern political parties in the US. He mostly agrees with the party's core political and social objectives.

Dr. Tesfaye holds Barack Obama in the highest regard among Democratic Party leaders due to his many well-known accomplishments. First, he regarded him as the sagest and most practical leader of the US. He had a high degree of intellect to handle any critical national or international issue. For instance, unlike his predecessors, he controlled fundamentalism, terrorism, and militant Islamic movements with tact and intelligence.

Most international political experts agree with Dr. Tesfaye's conclusions about Obama's multilateral pragmatic internationalism to successfully address global concerns, including terrorism.

Fareed Zakaria, a well-known journalist and author who currently shows Fareed GPS on CNN, claims that Obama doesn't receive enough credit for improving America's standing worldwide. According to him, Obama has restored the US's reputation, and US leadership is now more popular.

"What opponents view as a retreat is actually the US regaining its post-9/11 war stance and, more crucially, Obama absorbing the tactical insights of the past decade. The indicators of American strength or leadership are neither a constant state of wartime mobilization nor a desire to participate in unwinnable military operations. They have more frequently made it more difficult to maintain the postwar liberal order, which has been the driving force behind our foreign policy victories for many years and will continue to be in the future."

The American political system is quite complicated. Even though constant inconsistencies characterize the system, it also provides efficient controls for dealing with them. Opportunities and racial obstacles conflict with one another. For instance, on one side, there are many chances for all US residents to work and lead fulfilling lives, yet on the other, there are significant gaps in people's living standards.

Similar contradictions can be seen in the political sphere: the nation has best practices for protecting individuals' liberties and rights, but a racial problem still continues to be the country's most distinctive trait overall.

Chapter 16: Perspective on Humanity's Future Potential

The Future of Humanity and Technology

As a top-tier scientist, Dr. Tesfaye is convinced that technological advancements in many areas will significantly impact human progress in the future.

He believes if we consider the history of technological transformation, which dates back to ancient times, we can see that the significant changes currently occurring in the industry will unavoidably have an impact on humankind's future. The discovery of fire was a turning point in the development of technology. Another innovation that changed civilization was the use of fire for metalworking.

In addition, the development of cars and airplanes employing various metals dramatically influenced human existence. The other significant technical advancement in human life was the development of fax.

Today, with various forms of wireless technology, we may effortlessly contact anyone throughout the world. The lives of humans today and in the future will continue to change as a result of this progress.

Many experts in the area agree with Dr. Tesfaye's view regarding the unavoidable impact of technology on mankind in the future. The majority of technology researchers assert that no part of human existence has gone unaffected by technology.

The innovations that arose in the latter part of the 20th century dramatically altered every aspect of life, including industry, medicine, and how we work.

Additionally, according to Dr. Tesfaye, any country that wishes to keep up with the global change occurring at a rapid rate needs to progress its technology in all areas (such as in the fields of industries, communications, transportation, and health). The growth of technology is accelerating human development.

Scientists have already given this stage of technological advancement by humans the label "Tran humanism"—a movement that attempts to comprehend what constitutes a human being and how we might go beyond our inherent constraints. According to the movement, there is a need to improve our capacities, and any constraints on these capacities may be removed. What's more, it reckons that science and technology hold the secret to defeating them.

The theory of evolution of living things as depicted by Dr. Tesfaye is summerized below:

Plants and humans/mammals are vertical living things that evolved in different directions. Plants bury their roots (heads) in the ground and grow out thier branches upwards in to the air. However, humans/mammals keep their heads up in the air, but their hands and legs (branches) are pointed down towards the ground. They both feed thru their heads and breath thru their branches. In addition, they both feed upon each other. animals eat plants, and decayed bones and animal byproducts feed plants.

Fish and reptiles live horizontallt living things. However, birds are, in the air they prefer horizontal like fish and reptiles, but on the ground they dewell vertical like mammals.

This vertical - horizontal evolution is determined by adopting to the three phases of matter: solid (earth), liquid (water) and gas (air).

Part III: **DRUG DISCOVERIES, PUBLICATIONS AND PATENTS**

Chapter 17: Important Drug Discoveries by Dr. Tesfaye Biftu

Drug research has evolved over time as a result of intellectual ingenuity, intelligence, and talent, as well as the necessity to survive and ensure the survival of civilizations.

For these compounds to be used properly by the general public, knowledge of their historical development is necessary. The goal of drug research in the chemical, pharmaceutical, pharmacological, and biomedical sciences must be understood by novices to the subject.

Since 1805, isolated and chemically described pure, active, medicinal components have been discovered. Parallel to these advancements, the knowledge of human anatomy, physiology, biochemistry, genetics, and pharmacology has evolved. There were some new synthetic medicines found.

The chemistry of scents and sensory processes, such as memory, were clarified.

Emerging researchers now have access to these alternative therapies thanks to the legacy of exciting discoveries produced by Nobel Prize-winning scientists.

Drug development research with a broader scope investigates all aspects of drug development, from target discovery and validation to the relationships between structure and activity through post-market clinical reporting.

Drug development involves a collaborative effort from pharmacologists, pharmacists, toxicologists, medicinal, pharmaceutical, and organic chemists, chemical and molecular biologists, and drug review, authorization, and regulation experts.

Whatever specialty anyone picks, it is important to remember that the most significant breakthroughs can only be made if different disciplines are combined into a continuum that encompasses all critical processes in developing a new medicinal therapy.

The medicinal chemist must comprehend both the biological process and the physicochemical requirements for an effective drug formulation. Pharmaceutics deals with selecting the best medicine delivery method based on the condition that has to be treated.

Pharmaco-genomics is relevant at every stage, from the confirmation of therapeutic targets to the ultimate approval for clinical usage. Choosing a niche in drug research and development while keeping a broad viewpoint and a variety of career opportunities may be the most desirable feature for a budding scientist to explore this field.

Additionally, someone with a solid understanding of drug development might pursue careers in fields unrelated to research, such as working for governmental organizations, patent offices, investment businesses, and more. Few professions provide the same options for young scientists who drive to make a difference in a crucial issue - our health.

Dr. Tesfaye spent 35 years working in the pharmaceutical and biotechnology industries. This section includes a few of his short anecdotes regarding drug development during that time. It covers work done between 1981 and 1993 and 1995 and 2016 at the New Jersey-based multinational pharmaceutical company Merck & Co.

It also covers his work done during his two-year break from Merck from 1993 to 1995. He also worked at Cytomed Inc., a biotechnology company in Cambridge, Massachusetts.

Dr. Tesfaye worked in academics before joining Merck in 1981. His academic study focused on the synthesis and structural analysis of natural compounds. His initial project after joining Merck in 1981 was with COX-1 inhibitors as anti-inflammatory medications.

In 1982, Dr. Tesfaye began research on the Interleukin-1 (IL-1) inhibitors project for inflammation. A year later, in 1983, he began exploring Topoisomerase inhibitors as antibacterial drugs. Between 1983 and 1987, he worked on Platelet Activating Factor (PAF) receptor antagonists for asthma, thrombosis, and sepsis. Squalene synthase inhibitors as anti-cholesterol medications were the focus of Dr. Tesfaye's research between 1988 and 1992.

The next year, 1993, he relocated to Cambridge, Massachusetts, where he began working for Cytomed Inc., a newly founded biotechnology business that was researching dual Leukotriene-PAF inhibitors for asthma and nicotinic receptor agonists for illnesses of the central nervous system.

In 1995, Dr. Tesfaye rejoined Merck and started working on *beta*-3 Adrenergic Receptor Agonists to treat obesity. Until that point, his studies had mostly concentrated on human health. But in 1997, Dr. Tesfaye took over as the head of the Medicinal Chemistry team working on animal health.

Protein Kinase G (PKG) was identified as a disease target in chickens as an anti-coccidial anti-protozoan agent.

After coccidiosis, Dr. Tesfaye focused on DPP-4 inhibitors as anti-diabetic medications between 2000 and 2009. He worked on the Januvia®

team, a once-daily oral anti-diabetic medication, and led the Marizev® team, a once-weekly oral anti-diabetic medication.

Dr. Tesfaye worked on three separate initiatives in 2011, all of which blossomed into successful discovery projects. These treatments included GPR40 receptor antagonists for diabetes, Thrombin Receptor Antagonists (TRA) for thrombosis, and Direct Thrombin Inhibitors (DTi) for thrombosis. The GPR40 programmes covered both once-daily and once-weekly dosage. He worked with others on the CGRP migraine study from 2012 to 2014.

One of the molecules created for this programme, Ubrogepant®, which has a DPP-4 back up programme side chain, was chosen as a clinical candidate and subsequently licenced out to Allergan, a multinational pharmaceutical company with its headquarters in Ireland. Later, in December 2019, it received approval from the US Food and Drug Administration.

From this initiative, a number of clinical candidates were also produced, but none of them made it to the commercial stage.

The history of the aforementioned projects will be discussed in this chapter, along with the issues Dr. Tesfaye encountered and the resolutions he found throughout his investigation.

CYCLOOXYGENASE INHIBITORS FOR INFLAMMATION

Pathogens in the environment, such as bacteria and viruses, as well as physical traumas, naturally cause inflammation in the body. The activation of the complement cascade is the root cause of chronic inflammatory disorders. The complement system first becomes active in response to bacteria, viruses, or other antigens. During the activation phase, leukocytes are drawn to the inflamed area, where they consume immune complexes and release hydrolyzing enzymes.

When these potent hydrolyzing enzymes are released, tissue and cartilage are damaged. It is impossible to treat inflammation. The majority of available medications are palliative, meaning they just treat the symptoms rather than the underlying cause of the condition.

Swelling at the location of the inflammation, discomfort, and fever are indicators of inflammation.

The basic mechanism for combating inflammation involves blocking the Arachidonic Acid (AA) cascade. This triglyceride is hydrolyzed by the enzyme phospholipase A2 and produces AA, which is then oxidized by two other kinds of enzymes. Leukotrienes (LT), which cause respiratory illnesses, including asthma, are produced as a result of oxidation by the enzyme lipoxygenase.

Alternately, oxidation by cyclooxygenases (COX) produces intermediate peroxides, which go through a process of rearrangement to produce several types of inflammatory prostaglandins (PGs), which are depicted in red, and prostacyclin, which is seen in green.

Controlling the quantity of acid released during digestion is facilitated by prostacyclin. Therefore, inhibiting the cyclooxygenase enzyme prevents the synthesis of both the beneficial prostacyclin and the harmful prostaglandin.

Before the 1960s, steroids were the medication of choice, although they are associated with a number of adverse effects. The cyclooxygenase enzyme is inhibited by non-steroidal anti-inflammatory drugs (NSAIA), such as aspirin and naproxen. NSAIAs work effectively to reduce edema, fever, and discomfort.

They do, however, lead to stomach ulcers. GI bleeding brought on by NSAIA causes a number of fatalities each year. As a result, drug research laboratories focused the majority of their efforts in the 1980s on developing medications that have few adverse effects on the stomach and reduce fever, swelling, and discomfort.

When designing drugs in the 1970s and 1980s, Dr. Tesfaye and his colleagues did not employ computer modeling or X-rays of target proteins or substrates. They developed new compounds by manually creating physical models of substrates and superimposing them on medicinal molecules.

They also used force field calculations to establish the best torsion angles between bonds. The medication Indomethacin®, seen in red on the schematic above, was placed over the 20-carbon AA, which is indicated in black. The left-side lipophilic groups were well overlaid, as were the center and right-hand acid groups.

Dr. Tesfaye found Candidate 1 as an anti-inflammatory drug in 1981 after going through these exercises. Candidate 1 is about five times more potent than Indomethacin®, yet it has lower ulceroginicity and 90% less GI discomfort.

- X 5 potency vs. Indocin
- X 90 GI safety vs. Indocin (WHY ???)
- Activity resides in the (-)enantiomer*

At that time, they were unable to explain why a very strong COX1 inhibitor caused less gastrointestinal tract discomfort.

Dr. Tesfaye started thinking about it once he entered academia and discovered that the right-hand sulfur is in charge of this great selectivity. Sulfur is more basic than oxygen but less basic than nitrogen. The sulfur of the methyl thio group is protonated in the stomach, where the pH is about one, making it inert against the target enzyme COX1 and preventing prostacyclin reduction.

However, the substance is a strong COX1 inhibitor once it enters the circulation and the synovial fluid, which has a pH of 6.8, where it inhibits PGs and lowers inflammation, pain, and fever. This was demonstrated by using the more ulcerogenic Chloro analogue rather than the methyl thio group, which cannot protonate in the presence of stomach acid.

TOPOISOMERASE INHIBITOR- Anti-Bacterial

During transcription and replication, the human DNA topoisomerase I enzyme helps to relax DNA's supercoiling. These enzymes catalyze the breaking and rejoining of the phosphodiesters that support DNA strands during the regular cell cycle, which regulates the changes in DNA wrapping and unwinding. These enzymes are thus targets for chemotherapeutic therapies for cancer. Topoisomerase inhibitors also have antimicrobial properties.

Bacterial topoisomerases are in charge of inserting negative supercoils into DNA as well as decatenation of DNA. This activity is carried out by quinolones, including ciprofloxacin. They attach to topoisomerase enzymes and block DNA replication, killing bacteria.

Toyoma Patent
E.Coli ug/mL 0.1

New Design
E. Coli ug/mL 0.05

Dr. Tesfaye began working on the Topoisomerase Inhibitors programme in 1983 with the goal of developing antibacterial drugs. When he entered the programme, a Japanese business named Toyama possessed a patent on a brand-new family of extremely strong topoisomerase inhibitors used as an antibacterial drug.

Tesfaye's task was to locate a unique structure that wasn't covered by the Toyama patent and would serve as the starting point for research on the link between structure and activity. They intended to safeguard the brand name of the antibacterial medication Norfloxacin® that was available at the time.

In his research, he considered the Toyoma lead to be four separate fragments, as illustrated in the middle of the design. By retaining three of the groups and altering one fragment at a time, Dr. Tesfaye created a few analogues. In Merck's history, this was the first attempt at fragment best lead identification.

A new bioisostere may be added in place of the carboxylic acid, or a spacer such as a methylene, ethylene, or propylene group might be added as a spacer while maintaining the three-ring fragments.

Through these tests, he found that the 4-pyridone core was the only piece that could be altered without losing the activity. The newly discovered 2-pyridone core, which was not protected by the Toyoma patent, ended up serving as their program's lead structure. Then he switched to a different program.

PLATELET ACTIVATING FACTOR

Platelet Activating Factor (PAF) antagonists have been discovered to have a number of therapeutic applications throughout the years. PAF contains an ether bond in the first position rather than the typical ester linkage. It possesses a short chain acetoxy group at the 2-position rather than the typical long chain fatty acid, which is crucial for PAF's biological action.

Sepsis, which results from an overreaction to infection, was the second possible PAF receptor antagonist indication. Its physiologic effects are remarkably similar to those of PAF, including anaphylaxis.

Additionally, it was concluded that PAF antagonists would be useful in the treatment of atherosclerosis.

Veraguinsen
J.Chem Soc., 1978, 1147

MK287 (Phase 2B);
Chem., 1986, 1917; 1992, 3474

Dr. Tesfaye shared a lab with a biologist, Dr. S. B. Hwang, who joined Merck from Berkeley University when he started working on this project. He took up one side of the lab while Dr. Tesfaye, the chemist, took up the other. Dr. Hwang created a PAF receptor binding test. However, for around six months, he unsuccessfully screened a number of compounds to find a lead candidate.

Dr. Hwang was primarily searching for a PAF-like phospholipid polar molecule, but none of them were active. Dr. Tesfaye created an analogue of the natural substance Veraguinsen while attending graduate school at Brandeis University, which he then published in the Journal of Chemical Society in 1978. Veraguinsen has a symmetrical structure with four chiral centers that might result in eight distinct isomers.

Veraguinsen's natural constituents must be accurately characterized by comparing spectral data with each of its eight isomers. Out of frustration, lacking active compounds from screening their chemical collection, one day, Dr. Tesfaye gave the biologist a sample of Verguinsen obtained from his professor for evaluation in the PAF receptor-binding assay.

It was found to be active, but nobody believed the results until the assay was repeated four more times. This became the beginning of a new program that lasted over 5 years. Dr. Tesfaye and his fellow worker started modifying Verguinsein. After several years we came up with MK-287 and its backup candidate 2, which were very potent PAF antagonists, safe in animal models, and active in rat, monkey, and sheep asthma models.

However, in Phase 2B human clinical studies, it did not show benefits in human asthmatic patients. At the time, Merck could not come up with an appropriate clinical trial design to test MK-287 in sepsis and atherosclerosis. Both these diseases are deadly if not treated within minutes. MK-287 was kept on the shelf, and no follow-up was attempted.

SQUALENE SYNTHASE INHIBITORS – Hypocholesterolemic Agents

Atherosclerosis and related heart diseases are strongly associated with elevated blood levels of total cholesterol. Due to the widespread incidence and severity of this pathological condition leading to heart attack or stroke, major efforts were made to discover and develop hypocholesterolemic agents.

The statins are HMG-CoA reductase inhibitors, and they block the action of the enzyme 3-hydroxy-3-methylglutaryl coenzyme A reductase (HMGR) which is the rate-limiting step of cholesterol biosynthesis. Merck manufactures one of these classes of successful drugs, Mevacor® (Lovastatin). This led us to the investigation and design of inhibitors of other downstream enzymes involved in the multistep cholesterol biosynthetic pathway shown in the below scheme.

Squalene synthase inhibitors were considered not to interfere with the biosynthesis of other downstream biologically important molecules, and thus we expected a better side-effect profile for these inhibitors. Screening began, and our natural products group identified zaragozic acid, a 2,8- dioxabicyclo[3.2.1]octane derivative from a fermentation broth of fungi collected from the Zaragoza river in Spain. Zaragozic acid was found to be a potent inhibitor of squalene synthase.

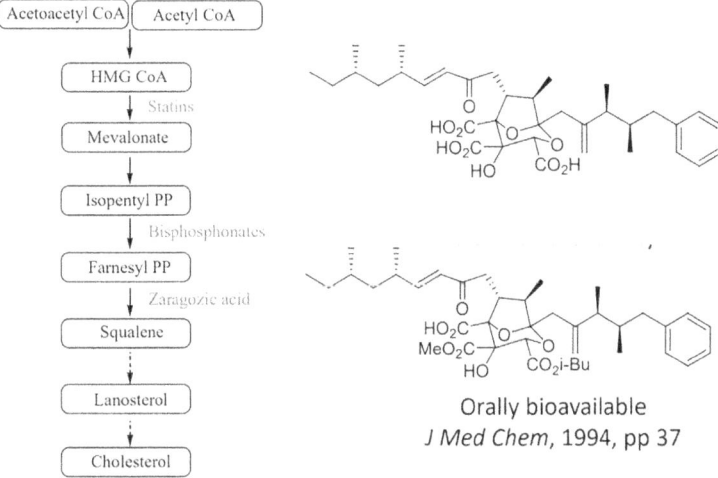

Orally bioavailable
J Med Chem, 1994, pp 37

However, the natural product was not biologically absorbed into the bloodstream and was not active when given orally. The assignment given to Dr. Tesfaye was to make it orally active.

Observation of the molecule that has three polar carboxylic acid groups suggests these polar acid groups could hinder oral absorption due to low lipophilicity.

So, Dr. Tesfaye decided to make six analogs of zaragozic acid: three mono-methyl esters at each acid position, three di-esters, and one tri-ester.

When dosed orally, the 1,2-diester showed good enzyme activity and oral bioavailability. They then started making several diester analogs to further optimize the lead. The 1-t-butyl, 2-methyl ester was chosen as a lead candidate.

NICOTINIC AGONISTS: Tourette's, Parkinson's, Alzheimer's, and others.

Epipedobates tricolor, a species of poisonous frog native to Ecuador, is where epibatidine was originally discovered. It has been demonstrated that this alkaloid has a strong analgesic effect with a nonopioid mode of action.

Epibatidine had an analgesic effect that was 200 times greater than morphine in the hot plate assay and 500 times more than morphine in triggering the Straub-tail reaction.

In both rats and mice, the hot-plate or tail-flick test has shown that nicotine, a ganglionic and skeletal muscle receptor agonist, has a strong analgesic effect on heat stimuli.

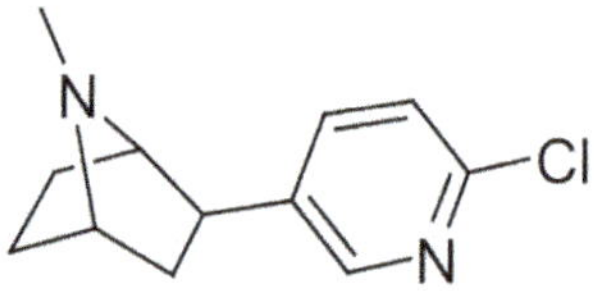

Epibatidine

The activation of nicotinic receptors, which are ligand-gated ion channels, results in fast increases in the permeability of cells to Na+ and K+ as well as depolarization and excitation.

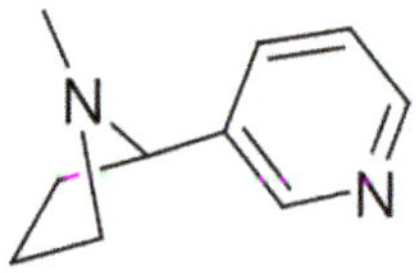

Nicotine

When Dr. Tesfaye joined Cytomed Inc. in Cambridge, Massachusetts, in 1994, the group was working on analogues of epibatidine that may be used to treat conditions including obesity, ulcerative colitis, smoking, Parkinson's, Alzheimer's, and Tourette's syndrome, as well as other conditions.

The mode of action, however, was unknown to them. Dr. Tesfaye proposed testing epibatidine in a nicotinic receptor assay because of the structural resemblance to nicotine. With an IC50 of 70 pM, it was examined and discovered to be the most potent nicotinic receptor agonist ever discovered. They started the structural modification process with a group at the University of Virginia led by Dr. T.Y. Shen.

Objectives were to modify the bridgehead nitrogen in an attempt to avoid mutagenicity of nicotine and the 3-pyridyl hetcrocycle.

Their rationale for the potential disease indications was as follows: Many epidemiology reports have found that smokers are less likely to develop Parkinson's disease than non-smokers.

A clinical condition called Parkinsonism includes bradykinesia, stiffness of the muscles, resting tremors, and abnormalities in posture and gait. There is a lot of data that points to Parkinsonism as a condition caused by a dopaminergic innervation deficit in the basal ganglia.

Blocking cholinergic activity is a second method of treating Parkinson's disease in an effort to balance the tone of the dopaminergic and cholinergic systems in the striatum. Tourette's Syndrome, a different movement disease, appears to be sensitive to nicotine.

Therefore, based on this discovery, nicotine agonists may have use as anti-obesity medications. By substituting other 5, or 6-membered aromatic heterocycles for the 3-pyridyl group, DR. Tesfaye and his colleagues were able to find a number of analogues with profiles that were equivalent to or better than those of epibatidine.

β3 ADRENERGIC RECEPTOR AGONISTS AS ANTI-OBESITY AGENTS

There are three subclasses of adrenoceptors: 1, 2, and 3. The main effect of stimulating the 1 adrenergic receptor (1 AR) is an increase in heart rate, whereas stimulating the 2 adrenergic receptor (2 AR) often causes bronchodilation and smooth muscle relaxation. Atypical receptors, now known as 3 adrenergic receptors (3 AR), are located on the cell surface of both white and brown adipocytes, where their activation stimulates both lipolysis and energy expenditure. These receptors are involved in adipocyte lipolysis.

Alkyl urea substituted Benzenesulfonamide derivatives were known to be potent and selective agonists of the human β3 AR. However, many of these compounds lacked good oral bioavailability.

So, when Dr. Tesfaye joined the anti-obesity program in 1997, my primary assignment was to identify benzenesulfonamides analogs with improved oral bioavailability. They discovered the replacement of the alkyl urea with benzyl and phenoxymethylene substituted oxadiazoles provided potent, selective, and orally bioavailable β3 AR agonists. The 4-trifluoromethoxy and 3,4 difluoro substituted benzyl oxadiazole (Candidate 3) has an EC50 of 8 nM in the β3 AR agonist assay with 100-fold selectivity over β1 and β2 AR binding inhibition activity. In dogs, its oral bioavailability is over 30%, with a half-life of 3.8 in 0.4 h.

In anesthetized rhesus monkeys, it evoked a dose-dependent glycerolemia (ED50Gly=0.15 mg/kg). Under these conditions, we observed a heart rate increase of 15% at a dose level of 10 mg/kg. These groups of compounds have good oral bioavailability and in vivo activity. As such, these heterocyclic analogs were selected and used as tools to evaluate the role of β3 receptor agonists in obesity and diabetes. Later on, follow-up by the team resulted in a repurposed use of one of the analogs for bladder control, marketed as Vebegron ®.

PROTEIN KINASE G INHIBITORS - Anticoccidial Agents

In 1999, Dr. Tesfaye transitioned from human health research to animal health research. Animal health research has three categories: companion animals such as dogs and cats, food animals such as chickens, cows, and sheep, and other sports animals such as horses and mules, which in developing countries are used for transportation.

In the US, over 30 billion chickens are raised on farms every year and consumed. A large number of chickens, usually 10,000- 20,000, are confined to a very small area in most poultry production facilities.

Coccidiosis is a contagious parasitic protozoan infection closely related to malaria disease. It is specifically caused by the Eimeria species, which are intracellular parasites - meaning that the parasites penetrate and live inside the host cell. All major poultry operations use anticoccidial agents on a prophylaxis basis, and apply the treatment before the chickens are infected.

The feed that is given to chickens is formulated with anticoccidial agents. In the past 40 years, there was no new anticoccidial agent introduced to the market. As a result, the parasites have developed some resistance to the old medications, so there's an urgent need to discover a new anticoccidial agent.

In addition, since about 30 million chickens are consumed annually, to reduce the cost of poultry production and thereby reduce the price of poultry meat, the cost of treatment has to be kept below five cents per chicken for the whole duration of the treatment period, i.e., 42 days.

To discover a better and more effective anticoccidial agent, the biology team developed a new cell-based petri-dish screening assay using some species of the parasites.

Several hundred thousand compounds were screened, and the pyrrole analog Compound 1 was identified as a very potent lead compound. It has nano-molar range activity against four different species of parasites in vitro. Later, when this compound was put in the feed, it effectively eliminated the parasites in live chickens.

Compound 1

At the time, the mechanism of the anticoccidial activity of Compound 1 was not known. To investigate the mechanism, Dr. Tesfaye and the radio-synthesis team synthesized the radio-labeled analog of Compound 1 and then the biology team incubated it with proteins extracted from the parasite.

The protein, which binds to Compound 1, was investigated and found to be a cyclic GMP-dependent protein kinase, PKG (JBC, 15913, 2002). The newly isolated PKG was then cloned and expressed. The binding site was found to be the kinase ATP site, and compound 1 was found to displace ATP in a competitive manner.

The parasite PKG is very distinct or different from chicken and other mammalian parasites, allowing the destruction of the parasite without affecting the chicken.

They optimized Compound 1 against PKG for about a year or two and came up with two potential candidates.

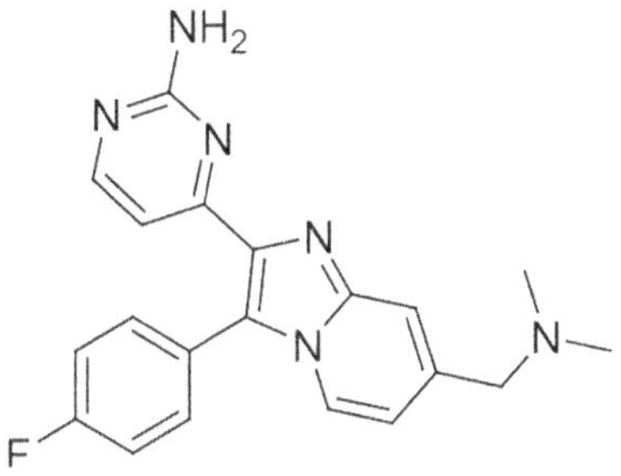

Candidate 4

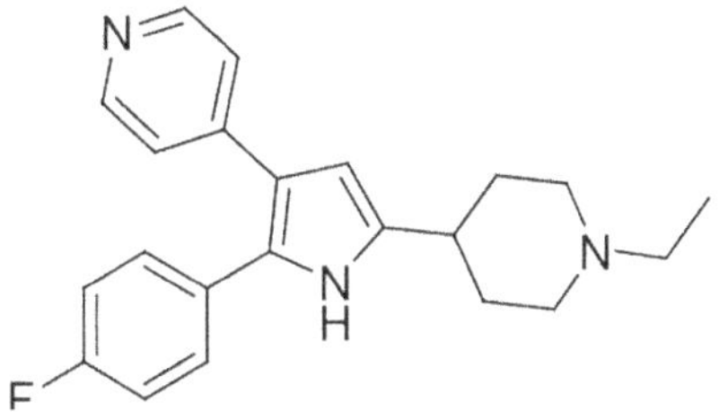

Candidate 5

Candidate 4 is a very potent PKG inhibitor with 0.1 nano molar activity. When this compound is added to chicken feed, it clears or kills the entire parasite at less than 15 ppb.

It has a wide spectrum of activity against various strains and does not have any antibacterial activity. A good anti-protozoan product should not have any antibacterial activity to avoid resistance. In addition, the cost of production was less than five cents per chicken during the 42 days duration of feed. Candidate 5 meets all the required criteria for a product candidate.

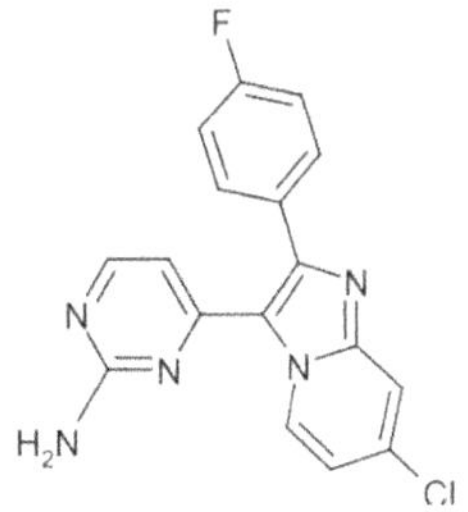

Candidate 6

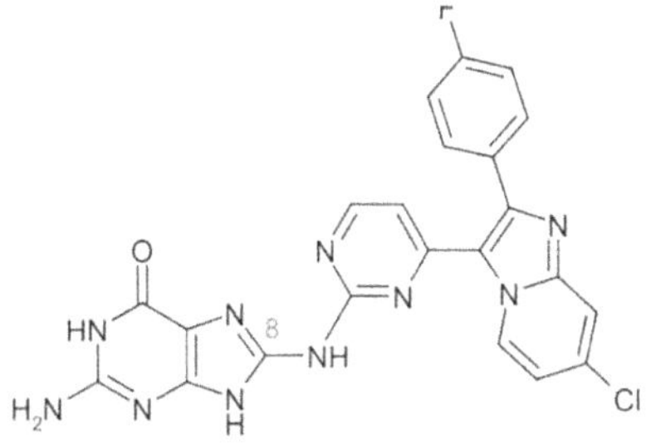

Guanine adduct A

Further investigation showed that the amino group attached to the 2-pyrimidine ring was the reason why L-417 was Ames positive. The amino group could be oxidized to hydroxylamine and further transformed into an iminium intermediate that could covalently bind to DNA upon decomposing.

This was confirmed by incubating radio labeled Candidate 4 with guanine and recovering the adduct formed. Candidate 5 was abandoned from further development.

In parallel, they were also investigating the parole lead Compound 1 and from this lead Candidate 5 was identified with excellent potency and was Ames negative. So, Candidate 6 was selected as the lead development candidate. Here's the summary of the activity relationship of Candidate5.

Structure diagram with annotations:
- 4-pyridyl essential
- Hydrogen preferred
- piperidine is most potent
- Basic amine essential
- 4-F essential; 2 and 3-substitution tolerated
- pyrroles and oxazoles are active; 6 membered heterocycles are inactive; N-substitution not tolerated

DPP-4 INHIBITORS AS ANTI-DIABETIC AGENTS – DISCOVERY OF SITAGLIPTIN BACK-UP CLINICAL CANDIDATE

GLP-1 and its analogs has been the subject of intense research related to the treatment of type 2 diabetes. However, active GLP-1 (GLP-1[7–36] amide) is rapidly degraded in vivo through the action of dipeptidyl peptidase IV (DPP-4), a serine protease which cleaves a dipeptide from the N-terminus to give the inactive GLP-1[9–36]amide. Small molecule inhibitors of DPP-4 have been shown to prolong the beneficial effects of this incretin hormone, as well as stabilize other incretin hormones such as glucose-dependent insulinotropic polypeptide (GIP).

Dr. Tesfaye's initial assignment in this program was to identify a selective DPP8 inhibitor to determine the importance of selectivity of DPP4 against DPP-4. He and his team identified a selective DPP-8 inhibitor which was shown to be clearly toxic in animal models. This was highlighted as the major reason for the success of the DPP-4 program at Merck in Dr Peter Kim, President of Merck Research labs, retirement letter to employees. Dr. Tesfaye then led the DPP-4 team and his assignment was to identify a backup clinical candidate for sitagliptin, which at the time was in Phase 2 clinical trials and was later approved by the FDA in October 2006.

Sitagliptin has an IC50 of 18 nM in the DPP-4 assay. They replaced the triazolopiperazine of difluoro analog of sitagliptin with various ring size cyclic amides such as imidazolone, piperazolone, and diazepanone analogs. Diazepanone is the most potent compound in this series and has slightly better activity than sitagliptin.

DPP-4			
IC_{50}, nM	160	89	14

They investigated the activities of the four possible stereoisomers of the diazepanone analogs. The decreasing order of DPP-4 inhibitory activity is: (R,R) > (R,S) > S,S) > (S,R). The most potent isomer, (R,R), was then elaborated further by modifying the methyl adjacent to the carbonyl group of the diazepanone ring.

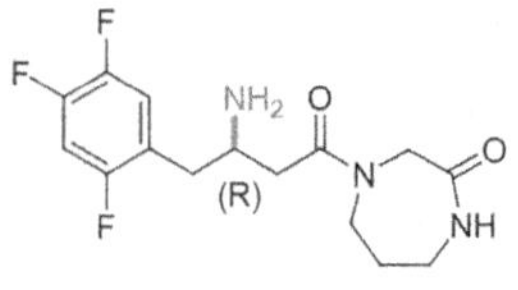

DPP-4 IC₅₀ = 140 nM 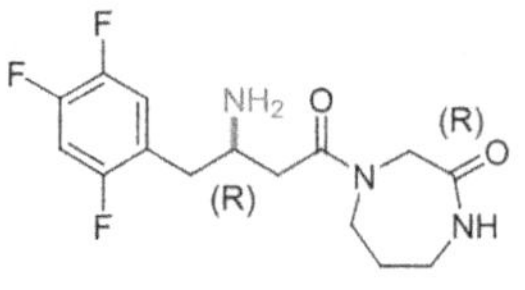
DPP-4 IC₅₀ = 6.6 nM 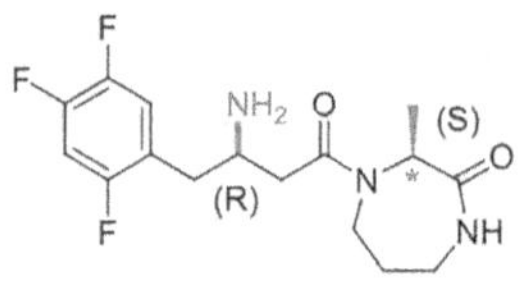
DPP-4 IC₅₀ = 150 nM
DPP-4 IC₅₀ = 403 nM 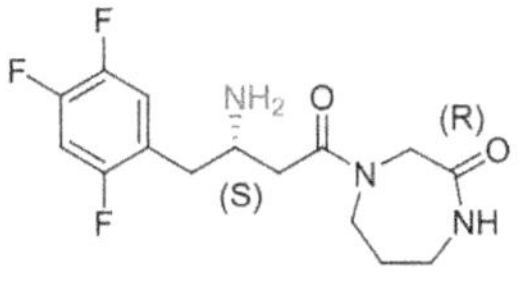
DPP-4 IC₅₀ = 67,000 nM 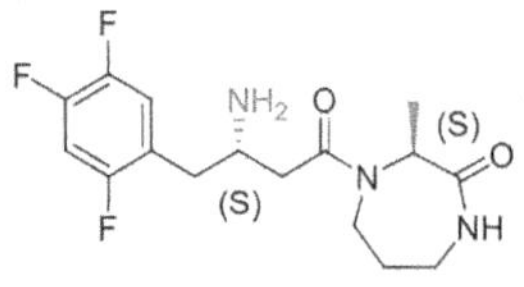
DPP-4 IC₅₀ = 2,300 nM

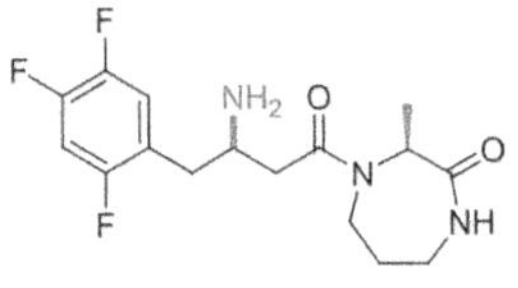

Structure-Activity-Relationship, and biological evaluation of (3R)-4-[(3R) 3 amino-4-(2,4,5-trifluorophenyl)butanoyl]-3-(2,2,2-trifluoroethyl)-1,4-diazepan-2-one, was chosen for extensive pre-clinical studies as a structurally diverse, potent, selective, orally efficacious, metabolically stable potential back-up to sitagliptin which has an excellent PK profile in diverse animal species.

NEW GENERATION DPP-4 INHIBITORS - OMARIGLIPTIN

The main objective of the new generation DPP-4 inhibitors program was to identify a specific DPP-4 inhibitor with a clinical advantage over sitagliptin. Dr. Tesfaye sought to have better potency, to keep dosage low, a long half-life (human predicted t1/2 >40 h) suitable for once weekly (QW) dosing to improve medication adherence, and structural diversity compared to other DPP-4 inhibitors in the market.

At the time Dr. Tesfaye embarked on solving these problems, the crystal structure of sitagliptin, depicted in yellow in the picture below, embedded in DPP-4 had been solved. Modeling of various middle amide linker substitution with diverse rigid rings showed that a six-member ring – cyclohexylamine (green), was an ideal candidate.

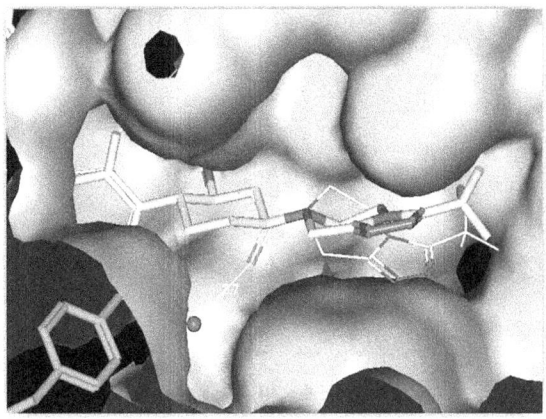

The cyclohexylamine analogs are potent and selective against other related proteases with excellent pharmacokinetic profiles. However, they block the human potassium channel hERG (human-ether-a-go-go related gene) at low micromolar concentrations. This has the pharmacological result of prolonging QTc (a measure of the time between the start of the Q wave and the end of the T wave in the heart's electrical cycle) in a cardiovascular dog model (CV-dog). Replacement of the cyclohexylamine with tetrahydropyran reduced the pKa of the primary amine from 8.6 to 7.3, and the hERG selectivity improved accordingly (IC50 = 23μM). In addition, the pyran analog was devoid of any QTc prolongation in the CV dog model at doses up to 30 mg/kg iv.

hERG IC$_{50}$ = 4,000 nM   hERG IC$_{50}$ = 23,000 nM

The observed pyrrolopyrimidine metabolite had weaker potency in DPP-4 (IC50 = 140 nM) and reduced selectivity against related proteases, QPP (IC50 = 160nM).

Several attempts were made to circumvent the metabolism on the right-hand-side amine. Attempts to block the oxidation sites with gem-dimethyl groups gave compounds with much reduced potency.

Pyrrolopyrazole gives compounds with good potency and selectivity. In addition, it was found to be stable and no oxidation product was observed when dosed in rats or dogs.

Since the best analog in the series has three chiral centers, all of the possible eight stereoisomers were made and evaluated in the DPP-4 and counter assays. The 2R,3S,5R isomer was found to be the most potent isomer. The trans-2,5-difluorophenyl-3- amino group is essential for binding to the DPP-4 protein active site.

2R, 3S, 5R
IC$_{50}$ 1.4 nM
Compound 1

2R, 3S, 5S
IC$_{50}$ 56 nM

2S, 3R, 5S
IC$_{50}$ 25,000 nM

2S, 3R, 5S
IC$_{50}$ 38,030 nM

2S, 3R, 5R
IC$_{50}$ 2,800 nM

2S, 3S, 5S
IC$_{50}$ 26,580 nM

2R, 3R, 5S
IC$_{50}$ 13,140 nM

2R, 3R, 5R
IC$_{50}$ >100,000 nM

Replacement of the 2-pyrazole hydrogen with the methylsulfonyl group resulted in omarigliptin (MK-3102). Omarigliptin was approved in

Japan for once weekly oral dosing in September 2015 and Marketed as Marizev®. Omarigliptin is:

- Highly potent, selective orally bioavailable.
- Efficacy, safety, and tolerability similar to sitagliptin.
- Achieves and maintains glycemic control in QW dosing.
- Potential for improved compliance and adherence.

In human oral dosing, 25 mg and 10 mg once weekly QW behaved similarly to daily dosing of 100 mg sitagliptin.

ADENOSINE MONOPHOSPHATE (AMP) ACTIVATED KINASE ACTIVATOR – MK8722

AMP-Activated Protein Kinase (AMPK) is a key regulator of mammalian energy homeostasis and has been implicated in mediating many of the beneficial effects of exercise and weight loss including lipid and glucose trafficking.

When Dr. Tesfaye was asked to join this project, his team was assigned to identify a potent, direct, allosteric activator of all twelve mammalian AMPK complexes for clinical evaluation.

At the time, the lead compound of the previous group had a candidate, benzoic acid derivative MK3903, which

- lacked potency against two of the subtypes
- showed undesirable activity against the ancillary assays such as CY2C/8/9
- had low oral bioavailability and high protein binding activity which resulted in a high oral dose and low tissue distribution, especially to muscle tissues.

Dr. Tesfaye and his team first converted the acid to a primary alcohol and the benzene to a cyclohexyl ring.

To reduce oxidation of the alcohol, the cyclohexyl was changed to hydroxy tetrahydropyran. After several investigations with other ring systems such as tetrahydrofuran, they discovered MK-8722, which met all the required criteria.

Short-acting pharmacologic AMPK activators, like long-acting ones, induce a pattern of gene expression in skeletal muscle, heart, liver and adipose tissues in rodents that is highly concordant to the effect of moderately strenuous exercise, a transcriptional resonance that occurred despite differences from exercise in respective acute substrate utilization.

A pharmacologic approach of daily short-acting AMPK activation acts as an exercise mimetic. Studies were conducted to compare the transcriptome responses in skeletal muscle, heart, liver, and white and brown adipose to small molecule activators of AMPK (pan-activators for all AMPK isoforms) compared to that of exercise.

Treadmill based running by lean mice activated muscle AMPK and reduced liver glycogen. In contrast, acute pharmacologic AMPK activation (under sedentary conditions), using a long-acting compound, acted to increase muscle glycogen more than 2-fold, in heart by more than 3-fold, and with less mobilization of hepatic glycogen than exercise.

Though pharmacologic AMPK activation mimics many of the cellular actions signaled by exercise, the effect on glycogen balance is quite different from exercise, though the effects on gene transcription displayed a striking concordance between exercise and pharmacologic AMPK activation.

GPR40 AGONISTS ANTI-DIABETIC AGENTS

GPR40 is a cell-surface GPCR that is highly expressed in human (and rodent) islets as well as in insulin-secreting cell lines.

Under hyperglycemic conditions, GPR40 agonists are capable of augmenting the release of insulin from islet cells. The specificity of this response is suggested by results showing that the inhibition of GPR40 activity by siRNA attenuates FA-induced amplification of GSIS.

These findings indicate that, in addition to the intracellular generation of lipid-derivatives of FA's that are thought to promote insulin release, FA's (and other synthetic GPR40 agonists) may also act as extracellular ligands that bind to GPR40 in mediating FA-induced insulin secretion.

There are several potential advantages of GPR40 as a potential target for the treatment of Type 2 Diabetes:

- GPR40- mediated insulin secretion is glucose dependent, there is little or no risk of hypoglycemia.
- The limited tissue distribution of GPR40 (mainly in islets) suggests that there would be less chance for side effects associated with GPR40 activity in other tissues.
- GPR40 agonists that are active in the islets may have the potential to restore or preserve islet function.

Long-term diabetes therapy often leads to the gradual diminution of islet activity, so that after extended periods of treatment, it is often necessary to treat Type 2 Diabetic patients with daily insulin injections.

By restoring or preserving islet function, GPR40 agonists may delay or prevent the diminution and loss of islet function in a Type 2 Diabetic patient.

MK-2305 has been reported as a potent and selective partial GPR40 agonist, in diabetic Goto Kakizaki rats decreased fasting glucose after acute and chronic treatment.

Dr. Tesfaye and his group worked on improving potency, half life and efficacy of MK-2305, MK-8666, and discovered severed compounds with desirable biological and physico-chemical properties for a once daily and once weekly dosing.

THROMBIN RECEPTOR INHIBITORS PAR1

Protease-activated receptors (PAR) are a subfamily of related G protein-coupled receptors that are activated by cleavage of part of their extracellular domain.

At the time DR. Tesfaye joined the project, Zontivity (Vorapaxar), a natural product PAR-1 inhibitor, was undergoing an advanced phase III clinical trial for acute coronary syndrome and secondary prevention of cardiovascular events. They also had a back-up program to address several objectives, namely, the long half-life of Vorapaxar, retinal vaculation events in rats, and hERG signals. Dr. Tesfaye and his team discovered several patentable new analogs. Among those, Candidate 7 was considered as a clinical candidate.

Vorapaxar SCH 590709 Candidate 7

S. Chackalamannil et. al

Candidate 7 met all the required criteria. It had the following properties:

PPB (Unbound %)		CYP RI IC50 (µM)		$t_{1/2}$ h		F%	
Rat	20.5	3A4	>50	Rat	2	Rat	54
Dog	16.8	2D6	>50	Dog	17	Dog	100
Monkey	16.6	2C9	>50	Cyno	20 (ter)	Cyno	37
Human	12						

Preliminary predicted human half-life $t_{1/2}$ 20 to 48 hr
Telemetry study (rat) Clean @ 10 and 30 mg / kg
SLO (30 mg/kg) Cyp3a23/3a1 (2.93 vs 1.0) and (Cyp7 3.6 vs 1.1)

DIRECT THROMBIN INHIBITORS

Direct Thrombin Inhibitors (DTIs) are a class of medications that act as anticoagulants (delaying blood clotting) by directly inhibiting the enzyme thrombin (factor IIa). One example of DTI in clinical use is Pradaxa.

After briefly leading a Thrombin Receptor Antagonists program, priority was shifted towards a Direct Thrombin Inhibitor program. Early DTI studies identified, (S)-N-(2-(aminomethyl)-5- chlorobenzyl)-1-((R)-2-hydroxy-3,3- dimethylbutanoyl)pyrrolidine-2-carboxamide-compound 2. We optimized the P3 group and identified novel, low molecular weight thrombin inhibitors.

Heterocycle replacement of the hydroxyl functional group maintained thrombin in vitro potency while improving the chemical stability and pharmacokinetic profile. These modifications led to the identification of Compound 10, which showed excellent selectivity over related serine proteases as well as in vivo efficacy in the rat arteriovenous shunt.

Compound 10 exhibited significantly improved chemical stability and pharmacokinetic properties.

2
Thrombin K_i (nM) = 2.1 nM

10: R = Me, Thrombin K_i = 9.6 nM
12: R = Cl, Thrombin K_i = 11 nM

CGRP (Calcitonin Gene Related Peptide) RECEPTOR ANTAGONISTS

CGRP stands for Calcitonin Gene-Related Peptide. It is a 37 amino acid neuropeptide that is released around the brain. CGRP is widely expressed in peripheral and central nervous systems and its level is elevated in the jugular vein during migraine attacks.

When CGRP is released, it causes intense inflammation in the coverings of the brain (the meninges), and for most migraine patients, causes the pain associated with a migraine attack.

When CGRP is administered intravenously to a person diagnosed with migraines, within four hours, most of them will get migraine-like symptoms. The anti migraine drug Sumatriptan normalizes CGRP levels concomitantly with pain relief.

CGRP had two teams working at different sites. Dr. Tesfaye's team was mainly focused on modifying the lead compound at various positions.

Expansion of the right-hand side pyrrolidone ring, which was also used in his previous DPP-4 program, gave many analogs submitted by the second team.

Ubrogepatant ® (n = 1)

One of these, UBROGEPANT®, eventually was selected as a clinical candidate and was developed by Allergan. It has the same right-hand used for the DPP-4 backup studies used by Dr. Tesfaye and his team for Sitagliptin – Januvia™.

ISOCITRATE DEHYDROGENASE-1 (IDH1) INHIBITORS

Isocitrate Dehydrogenase (IDH) is a key enzyme involved in the conversion of isocitrate to α-ketoglutarate (α-KG) in the tricarboxylic acid cycle.

Mutations in IDH1 (cytosolic) and IDH2 (mitochondrial) have been identified in multiple cancer types including, but not limited to, glioma, glioblastoma multiforme, paraganglioma, supratentorial primordial neuroectodermal tumors, acute myeloid leukemia (AML), prostate cancer, thyroid cancer, colon cancer, chondrosarcoma, cholangiocarcinoma, peripheral T-cell lymphoma, and melanoma.

The mutations have been found at or near key residues in the active site: G97D, R100Q, R132H, H133Q, and A134D for IDH1, and R140 and R172 for IDH2. These mutant forms of IDH are believed to have a neomorphic activity, reducing alpha-ketoglutarate to 2-hydroxyglutarate (2- HG). In general, production of 2-HG is enantiospecific, resulting in generation of the D-enantiomer (also known as the R enantiomer or R-2-HG). Normal cells generally have low native levels of 2-HG, whereas cells harboring these mutations in IDH1 or IDH2 show significantly elevated levels of 2-HG.

High levels of 2-HG have also been detected in tumors harboring the mutations. High levels of 2-HG have been detected in the plasma of patients with mutant IDH containing AML.

IDH inhibitor monotherapy for R/R AML is efficacious and safe; however, there are problems, such as primary or acquired resistance. Clinical trials of IDH inhibitors combined with hypomethylating agents or standard chemotherapy for the treatment of R/R AML or newly diagnosed AML, as well as in post hematopoietic stem cell transplantation as maintenance therapy, are ongoing.

There is a continuing need for small molecule inhibitors of mutant IDH enzymes, or more specifically IDH1 enzymes, for the treatment of diseases and disorders associated with these enzymes.

Our studies were directed to tricyclic compounds of formula (I) which are inhibitors of one or more mutant IDH enzymes in the potential treatment or prevention of cancers in which one or more mutant IDH enzymes are involved.

Chapter 18: Dr. Tesfaye's Major Publications and Patents

Dr. Tesfaye's Pharmaceutical Patents

Dr. Tesfaye Biftu has discovered and patented more than 100 applications independently or in collaboration with others. The majority of them have been issued patents in the United States of America.

The American legal database system Justia lists all of Tesfaye Biftu's significant medical patents.

Throughout his time working at Merck Company, he developed most drugs. Meanwhile, he has also collaborated with CytoMed, Inc., Merial Limited, Synexis and other pharmaceutical businesses.

Eighty of the patents Tesfaye found and created are included in two categories in the Justia database. The first category consists of pharmaceuticals for which Tesfaye has received patent rights.

His medical inventions are particularly helping people win the battle against most prevalent diseases such as Type 2 diabetes, inflammatory diseases, heart attack, and cholesterol.

His beloved wife, Mrs. Tersit, witnesses that the source of Tesfaye's extraordinary achievements is his exceptional commitment and hard work. She says, *"Dr. Tesfaye is hardworking, extraordinarily committed, devoted, and persistent."* She adds, *"He has used all his time and energy for innovation and discovery in his profession. He has unreservedly committed his career to the company he has worked for.*

"He usually outshines in international scientific forums, and his knowledge has been profound. He is always supportive and kind to people. He is not only socially active but also initiates different business ideas that benefit his friends and the community at large."

Dr. Tesfaye expresses his feelings regarding the drugs he has innovated so far, saying, *"I am thrilled and inspired when I think of the fact that the medicines whose discovery I have taken part in have provided relief to people suffering from illness."*

Major Publications by Dr. Tesfaye Biftu

Dr. Tesfaye Biftu has co-authored over 57 research articles published in the most prominent scientific journals. These articles are highly regarded in the medical profession and used as authoritative sources by university researchers.

Among these are articles co-authored with scholars who have played roles in his career development. Congressman Paul Todd is a case in point, and Professor Stevenson is another. With Congressman Todd, he co-authored articles entitled "TLC screening techniques for the qualitative determination of natural and synthetic capsaicinoids" published in the Journal of Chromatography Science (1975) and "Determination of pungency due to capsicum" published in the Journal of Food Science (1977), both reputable journals.

He co-authored three articles: "Flavone and triterpene constituents of Elaegia utilis" (1978), "Synthesis of the lignan (+)- deoxyschizandrin" (1978), and "Synthesis of lignans from 2,3-diaroylbutanes" (1978) with Dr. Stevenson, his former teacher and later colleague.

With Dr. Berhanu Abegaz, his former colleague at Addis Ababa University, co-authored an article titled "Fatty acid composition of Glynus lotoides, Sinet," published in the Ethiopian Journal of Science, 19-22 (1980).

Moreover, the outputs of his discoveries while working at Merck were also published in the form of great scientific discoveries.

A detailed list of the major scientific publications authored by Dr. Tesfaye is annexed at the end.

Dr. Tesfaye Biftu chiefly attributes his extraordinary achievement in medicinal chemistry to the support he got from different important people in his entire life.

"I was lucky to be supported by various people at different times in my life," he says.

"Among them are my father Aba Fira; my wife Tersit, Ato Tesfaye Admasu, a dedicated primary school teacher who inspired me at a young age by conducting scientific experiments; former Michigan Congressman Paul H. Todd; Kalsec vice-president Karl R. Sandelin, who invited me to the US and later supported my undergraduate education; and Professor Robert Stevenson of Brandeis University, who gave me guidance in my postgraduate studies and after that."

But there is no doubt he has qualities that have served him well in his career. He is an innovator who is constantly in search of new ideas and new ways of tackling old problems. While talented, he is also persistent and energetic in pursuing his goals.

Annex I: Sample Scientific Publications

Co-authored by Dr. Tesfaye Biftu

1. Houser, T., Biftu, T. and Hsieh, P.-F. (1975). Extraction rate equations for paprika and turmeric with certain organic solvents. J. Agric. Food Chem., 23(2), 353-355.

2. Todd, P., Bensinger, M. and Biftu, T. (1975). TLC screening techniques for the qualitative determination of natural and synthetic capsaicinoids. J. Chrom Sci., 13(12), 577-579.

3. Todd, P., Bensinger, M. and Biftu, T. (1977). Determination of pungency due to capsicum by GLC. J. Food Sci., 42(3), 669-665.

4. Biftu, T. and Stevenson, R. (1978). Flavone and triterpene constituents of Elaegia utilis. J. Chem Soc., Perkin 1, 360-363.

5. Biftu, T., Hazra, B. and Stevenson, R. (1978). Synthesis of the lignan (+)-deoxyschizandrin. J. Chem. Soc., Chem. Commun., 491-492.

6. Biftu, T., Hazra, B. and Stevenson, R. (1978). Synthesis of lignans from 2,3-diaroylbutanes. J. Chem. Soc., Perkin 1, 1147-1150.

7. Biftu, T., Hazra, B. and Stevenson, R. (1979). Synthesis of deoxyschizandrin and other lignans. J. Chem. Soc., Perkin 1, 2276.

8. Ph.D. Dissertation, Part 1. Synthetic routes to lignans; Part 2. Isolation and structure elucidation of constituents of Elaegia utilis. Brandeis University.

9. Tecle, B. and Biftu,T. (1980). Electroorganic synthesis of some natural product analogues Sinet: Ethiop. J. Sci. 3(1): 75

10. Biftu, T. and Abegaz, B. (1980). Fatty acid composition of Glynus lotoides. Sinet: An Eth. J. Sci., 19-22.

11. Houser, T., McCarville and Biftu, T. (1980). Kinetics of thermal decomposition of pyridine. Int. J. Chem. Kinetics, 12, 555.

12. Houser, T., McCarville and Biftu, T. (1980). Kinetics of formation of HCN during pyridine pyrolysis. Int. J. Chem. Kinetics, 12, 569.

13. Biftu, T. (1981). Essential oil composition of Aframoum korarima. JChrom., 211, 280.

14. Biftu, T., Schnieder, G. and Stevenson, R. (1982). Synthesis of quettamine alkaloid. J. Chem. Res., 10, 270.

15. Biftu, T. (1984). Synthesis and reduction of 5,5-dimethyl-2,4- bis(3,4-dimethoxyphenyl)-2-chloro-2,5-dihydrofuran. J. Het. Chem., 21, 881.

16. Biftu, T., Gamble, N., Hwang, S.-B., Shen, T. Y., Snyder, J., Springer, J., and Stevenson, R. (1986). Conformation and activity of tetrahydrofuran lignans as PAF antagonists. J. Med. Chem., 29(10), 1917.

17. Hwang, S.-B., Lam, M.-H., Biftu, T., Beattie, T. and Shen, T. Y. (1985). trans-2,5-bis(3,4,5-trimethoxyphenyl)tetrahydrofuran as PAF antagonist. J. Bio. Chem., 260(29), 1917.

18. Biftu, T. (1986). L-653150, A dual inhibitor of PAF & 5-LO.6th Int. Conf. on Prostaglandins, 302.

19. Doebber, T., Wu, M. and Biftu, T. (1986). Inhibition of PAFinduced in vivo responses by L-652731, a PAF receptor antagonist. J Pharm. & Exp. Therap., 239(3), 841.

20. Doebber, T., Wu, M. and Biftu, T. (1986). PAF mediation of rat anaphylactic responses to soluble immune complexes, studies with PAF antagonist L-652731. J. Immun., 136(12), 4659.

21. Chang, M. N., Biftu, T., Boulton, D. A., Finke, P. E., Hammond, M. L., Pessolano, A. A., Zambia, R. A., Bailey, P., Goldenberg, M., Rackham, A. (1986). Synthesis and analgesic activities of 2-(5-aroyl pyrrolo) alkanoic acids. Eur. J. Med. Chem., 21(5), 363.

22. Biftu, T. and Stevenson, R. (1987). Natural 2,5-bisaryltetrahydrofurans as platelet- activating factor antagonists. Phytotherapy Res., 97-106.

23. Ponpipom, M. M., Hwang, S. B, Doebber, T., Alberts, Biftu, T., Brooker, D., Bugianesi, R., Chabala, J. C., Gamble, N., Graham, D., Lam, M. H., and Wu, M. S. (1988). L-659989, A novel Potent PAF receptor antagonist. Biochem. Biophys. Res comm., 150, 1213-1220.

24. Biftu, T., Chabala, J. C., Acton, J., Beattie, T., Brooker, R., Bugianesi, R., Chang, M. N., Chiang, P.C., Gamble, N., Girotra, N., Graham, D., Kuo, C. H., Ponpipom, M., Sahoo, S., Shen, T. Y., Thompson, K. L., Yang, S. S., Hwang, S. B., and Doebber, T. (1988). Synthesis and SAR of 2,5-diaryltetrahydrofurans as PAF antagonists. Prostaglandins, 35(5), 846.

25. Biftu, T. Chabala, J., Acton, J., Kuo, H. C., and Stevenson, R. (1989). 2,5-Diaryltetrahydrofurans: PAF antagonists. Drugs of the future, 359-366.

26. Sahoo, S. P., Graham, D., Acton, J., Biftu, T., Bugianesi, R. L., Giorotra, N.G., Kuo, C-H., Ponpipom, M. M., Doebber, T. W., Wu, M. S., Hwang, S-B., Lam, M-H., MacIntyre, E., Bach, T. J., Luell, S., Meurer, R., Davies, P., Albert, A.W., Chabala, J. C. (1991). Synthesis and Biological Activity of MK-287, Biorg.and Med. Chem. Let., 327- 31

27. N. N. Girotra, T. Biftu, M. M. Ponpipom, J. J. Acton, A. W. Alberta, T. N. Bach, R. G. Ball, R. L. Bugianesi, W. H. Parsons, J. C. Chabala, P. Davies, T. W. Doebber, J. Doherty, D. W. Graham, S-B. Hwang, C. H. Kuo, M-H. Lam, S. Luell, D. E. MacIntyre, R. Meurer, C. D. Roberts, S. P. Sahoo, and M. S. Wu. (1992). L-680880-A-paf antagonist, J. Med. Chem., 35, 3474-3482

28. Wilson, K. E, Burk, R. M., Biftu, T., Ball, R. G., Hoogsteen, K. (1992). Zaragozic Acid A, A potent inhibitor of squalene synthase, J. Org. Chem., 57(26), 7151-58.

29. Chiang, P., Biftu, T. (1993). Diesters of Zargozic acid A, Biorg.& med.Chem.Lett., 2029

30. Kuo, H., and Biftu, T. (1993). Synthesis of C-3 Methyl Zaragozic acid A, TL, 34(43): 6863

31. Qian, C., and Biftu, T. (1933). Europ. J. Pharmacol., Epibatidine is a Nicotinic Analgesic, R13-14

32. Biftu, T., Acton, J-J, Berger, G-D, Bergstrom, J-D, Dufresne, C, Kurtz, M-M, Marquis, R-W, Parsons, W-H, Rew, D-R, Wilson, K-E (1994). SAR of Zaragozic acids, J. Med. Chem., 421

33. Biftu, T. (1995). Novel Antibacterial DNA Gyrase Inhibitors manuscript prepared but not submitted.

34. Biftu, T., Feng, D-D, Liang, G-B, Kuo, H, Qian, X, Naylor, E-M, Colandrea, V-J, Candelore, M-R, Cascieri, M-A, Colwell, L-FJr, Forrest,

M-J, Hom, G-J, MacIntyre, D-E, Stearns, R-A, Strader, C-D, Wyvratt, M-J, Fisher, M-H, Weber, A-E. (2000). Synthesis and SAR of Oxadiazoles benzenesulfonamides as Beta-3 agonist anti-obesity agents, Bioorg. Med. Chem. Lett., 10, 1432

35. Feng, D-D, Biftu,-T, Candelore, M-R, Cascieri,-M-A, Colwell, L-FJr, Deng, L, Feeney, W-P, Forrest, M-J, Hom, G-J, MacIntyre, D-E, Miller, R-R, Stearns, R-A, Strader, C-D, Tota,-L, Wyvratt, M-J, Fisher, M-H, Weber, A-E. (2000). Discovery of Orally bioavailable B-3 agonists, Bioorg. Med. Chem. Lett., 10, 1427.

36. Gurnett, A-M, Liberator, P-A, Dulski, P-M, Salowe, S-P, Donald, R.-G, Anderson, J-W, Wiltsie, J, Diaz, C-A, Harris, G, Chang, B, DarkinRattray, S-J, Nare, B, Crumley, T, Blum, P-S, Misura, A-S, Tamas, T, Sardana, M-K, Yuan, J, Biftu, T, Schmatz, D-M. (2002). Purification and Molecular Characterization of cGMP Dependent Protein Kinase from Apicomplexan Parasites: A Novel Chemotherapeutic Target, J. Bio. Chem, 227(18), 15913

37. Tamas, T., Biftu T, submitted to J. Parasitology, Anticoccidial Activity of a Novel PKG Inhibitor.

38. C. M. Brown, J. S. Mathew, T. Tamas, T. Biftu, D. R. Thompson. (2003). Isolation and characterization of a Diclazuril insensitive strain of Eimeria acervulina (Poster, World association for the advancement of Parasitology).

39. Kellerhouse, P. L., Mathew, J. S., Kersten, D., Brown, C. M., Biftu, T., and Thompson, D. R. (2003). Development of an in vitro culture system using Eimeria Tenella to evaluate the efficacy of anti-coccidial compounds. (American Association of Veterinary Parasitology).

40. Tesfaye Biftu, Dennis Feng, Mitree Ponpipom, Narindar Girotra, Gui-Bai Liang, Xiaoxia Qian, Robert Bugianesi, Joseph Simeone, Linda

Chang, Anne Gurnett, Paul Liberator, Paula Dulski, Penny Sue Leavitt, Tami Crumley, Andrew Misura, Terence Murphy, Sandra Rattray, Samantha Samaras, Tamas Tamas, John Mathew, Christine Brown, Don Thompson, Dennis Schmatz, Michael Fisher and Matthew Wyvratt. (2005). Synthesis and SAR of 2,3-Diarylpyrrole Protein Kinase G Inhibitors as Anticoccidial Agents, in press Bioorg. Med. Chem. Lett., 3296-3301

41. Gui-Bai Liang, Xiaoxia Qian, Tesfaye Biftu, Dennis Feng, Michael Fisher, Tami Crumley, Sandra J. Darkin-Rattray, Paula M. Dulski, Anne Gurnett, Penny Sue Leavitt, Paul A. Liberator, Andrew S. Misura, Samantha Samaras, Tamas Tamas, Dennis M. Schmatz, and Matthew Wyvratt. (2005). Hydroxylated N-Alkyl-4-Piperidinyl 2,3-Diarylpyrrole Derivatives as Potent and Broad-Spectrum Anticoccidial Agents, submitted to Bioorg. Med. Chem. Lett., 4570- 4573

42. Biftu, T., Feng, D. D., Fisher, M. H., Liang, G., Qian, X., Scribiner, A., Dennis, R., Lee, S., Brown, C. M., Gurnett, A. M., Leavitt, P. S., Liberator, P. A., Mathew, J. S., Misura, A. S., Samaras, S. D., Tamas, T., Schmatz, D. M., Wyvratt, M. J. (2006). Synthesis and SAR of very potent imidazopyridine antiprotozoan, in press. Bioorg. Med. Chem. Lett. 2079.

43. Feng, D., Fisher, M. H., Liang, G. B., Qian, X., Brown, C., Gurnett, A. M., Leavitt, P. S., Liberator, P. A., Mathew, J., Misura, A. S., Smamras, S., Tamas, T., Schmatz, D., Wyvratt, M. J., Biftu, T. (2006). Bioorg. Med. Chem. Lett. 5978.

44. Liang, G., Qian, X., Feng, D., Fisher, M., Brown, C. M., Gurnett A., Leavitt, P. S., Liberator, P. A. Misura, A. S., Tamas, T., Schmatz, D. M., Wyvratt, M. and Biftu, T. (2007). Synthesis and SAR studies of potent imidazopyridine anticoccidial agents. Bioorg. Med. Chem. Lett. 3558-3561.

45. Biftu, T., Dennis Feng, Xiaoxia Qian, Gui-Bai Liang, Gerard Kieczykowski, George Eiermann, Huaibing He, Barbara Leiting, Kathy Lyons, Aleksandr Petrov, Ranabir Sinha-Roy, Bei Zhang, Giovanna Scapin, Sangita Patel, Ying-Duo Gao, Suresh Singh, Joseph Wu, Xiaoping Zhang, Nancy A. Thornberry and Ann E. Weber. (2007). (3R)-4-[(3R)-3-Amino-4-(2,4,5-trifluorophenyl)butanoyl]- 3-(2,2,2-trifluoroethyl)-1,4-diazepan-2-one, a selective dipeptidyl peptidase IV inhibitor for the treatment of type 2 diabetes. Bioorg. Med. Chem. Lett. 49-52.

46. Gui-Bai Liang, Xiaoxia Qian, Dennis Feng, Tesfaye Biftu, George Eiermann, Huaibing He, Barbara Leiting, Kathy Lyons, Aleksandr Petrov, Ranabir Sinha-Roy, Bei Zhang, Joseph Wu, Xiaoping Zhang, Nancy A. Thornberry and Ann E. Weber. (2007). Optimization of 1,4-diazepan-2-one containing dipeptidyl peptidase IV inhibitors for the treatment of type 2 diabetes. . Bioorg.Med. Chem. Lett.1903-1907.

47. Biftu, T., Scapin, G., Singh, S., Feng, D.; Becker, J., Eiermann, G., He, H., Lyons, K., Patel, S., Petrov, A., Sinha-Roy, R., Zhang, B., Wu, J., Zhang, X., Doss, G., Thornberry, N., Weber, A (2007). Bioorg. Med. Chem. Lett. 3384-3387.

48. Gao, Y., Feng, D., Sheridan, R., Scapin, G., Patel, S., Wu, J.; Zhang, X., Sinha-Roy, R., Thornberry, N., Weber, A. Biftu, T. (2007). Bioorg. Med. Chem. Lett. 3877-3879.

49. Scribner, A., Dennis, R., Hong, J., Lee, S., McIntyre, D., Perrey, D., Feng, D., Fisher, M., Wyvratt, M., Leavitt, P., Liberator, P., Gurnett, A., Brown, C., Mathew, J., Thompson, D., Schmatz, D. Biftu, T. (2007). European Journal of Medicinal Chemistry, 42(11-12), 1334-1357.

50. Gui-Bai Liang, Xiaoxia Qian, Tesfaye Biftu, Suresh Singh, YingDuo Gao, Giovanna Scapin, Sangita Patel, Barbara Leiting, Reshma Patel, Joseph Wu, Xiaoping Zhang, Nancy A. Thornberry C., Ann E. Weber. (2008). Bioorganic & Medicinal Chemistry Letters 18 3706– 3710.

51. Liang, Gui-Bai; Qian, Xiaoxia; Feng, Dennis; Fisher, Michael; Crumley, Tami; Darkin-Rattray, Sandra J.; Dulski, Paula M.; Gurnett, Anne; Leavitt, Penny Sue; Liberator, Paul A.; Misura, Andrew S.; Samaras, Samantha; Tamas, Tamas; Schmatz, Dennis M.; Wyvratt, Matthew; Biftu, Tesfaye. (2008). Bioorganic & Medicinal Chemistry Letters, 18(6), 2019-2022.

52. Scribner, Andrew; Meitz, Susan; Fisher, Michael; Wyvratt, Matthew; Leavitt, Penny; Liberator, Paul; Gurnett, Anne; Brown, Chris; Mathew, John; Thompson, Donald; Schmatz, Dennis; Biftu, Tesfaye. Bioorganic & Medicinal Chemistry Letters (2008), 18(19), 5263-5267.

53. Scribner, Andrew; Dennis, Richard; Lee, Shuliang; Ouvry, Gilles; Perrey, David; Fisher, Michael; Wyvratt, Matthew; Leavitt, Penny; Liberator, Paul; Gurnett, Anne; Brown, Chris; Mathew, John; Thompson, Donald; Schmatz, Dennis; Biftu, Tesfaye. (2008). European Journal of Medicinal Chemistry. 43(6), 1123-1151.

54. Scribner, Andrew; Moore, Joseph A.,III; Ouvry, Gilles; Fisher, Michael; Wyvratt, Matthew; Leavitt, Penny; Liberator, Paul; Gurnett, Anne; Brown, Chris; Mathew, John; Thompson, Donald; Schmatz, Dennis; Biftu, Tesfaye. (2009). Bioorganic & Medicinal Chemistry Letters,. 19(5), 1517-1521.

55. Tesfaye Biftu, Xiaoxia Qian, Ping Chen, Dennis Feng, Giovanna Scapin, Ying-Duo Gao, Jason Cox, Ranabir Sinha Roy, George Eiermann, Huabing He, Kathy Lyons, Gino Salituro, Sangita Patel, Alexander Petrov, Feng Xu, Shiyao Sherrie Xu, Bei Zhang, Charles Caldwell, Joseph K. Wu, Kathy Lyons, Ann E. Weber. (2013). Novel tetrahydropyran analogs as dipeptidyl peptidase IV inhibitors: Profile of clinical candidate (2R,3S,5R)-2-(2,5-difluorophenyl)-5- (4,6-dihydropyrrolo[3,4-c]pyrazol-5-(1H)-yl)tetrahydro-2H-pyran-3- amine (23). Bioorg. Med. Chem. Lett. 23 5361–5366.

56. Timothy A. Blizzard, Sanjay Singh, Basanagoud Patil, Naresh Chidurala, Venukrishnan Komanduri, Samarpita Debnat, Sergei Belyakov, Alejandro Crespo, Alice Struck, Marc Kurtz, Judyann Wiltsi, Xun Shen, Lisa Sonatore, Marta Arocho, Dale Lewis, Martin Ogletree, Tesfaye Biftu. (2014). Heterocyclic core analogs of a direct thrombin inhibitor. Bioorg. Med. Chem. Lett. 24 1111–1115.

57. Omarigliptin – Once Weekly Anti-diabetic Agent, J Med Chem. (2014) 57, 3205

ANNEX II: Sample International Lectures by Tesfaye Biftu

1. Hwang, S. B., Biftu, T., Doebber, T. W., Lam, M. H., Wu, M. S. and Shen T. Y. A. 1985. Synthetic pseudolignan derivative as potent and specific PAF-acether antagonist. Symposium on "Is there a case for PAF?" Pasteur Institute, Paris, France, June.

2. Shen, T. Y., Hwang, S. B., Doebber, T., Biftu, T., Ponpipom, M., Bugianesi, R., Chang, M. N., Beattie, T. 1986. Lignan derivatives as PAF antagonists.6th Int. conference on prostaglandins and related compounds, Florence, Italy. June.

3. Biftu, T. (INVITED LECTURE), Gamble, N., Hwang, S.B., Chabala, J. C., Doebber, T., Dougherty, and Shen, T. Y. 1986. L-653150 A dual inhibitor of 5-Lipoxygenase and Platelet activating factor. 6th Int. conference on prostaglandins and related compounds, June.

4. Biftu, T. (INVITED LECTURE), Chabala, J. C., Acton, J., Beattie, T., Brooker, R., Bugianesi, R., Chang, M. N., Chiang, P. C., Gamble, N., Girotra, N., Graham, D., Kuo, C. H., Ponpipom, M., Sahoo, S., Shen, T. Y., Thompson, K. L., Yang, S. S., Hwang, S. B., and Doebber, T. (1988). Synthesis and SAR of 2,5-diaryltetrahydrofurans as PAF antagonists. Symposium on "There is a case for PAF", Pasteur Institute, Paris, France, May 1988.

5. Ip, S., Biftu, T. (1993). Pharmacological profile of THF as dual inhibitors of PAF and 5-LO, World congress on inflammation, Vienna, Austria, October.

6. Biftu, T. (2007). ACS 217th National Meeting, March1999, SAR of β-3 Agonists.

7. The Swedish Pharmaceutical Congress, Läkemedelskongressen October 22-24, 2007, City Conference Center, Folkets Hus, Stockholm, Sweden.

8. Societe Royale de Chemie 2007, New Drugs and Candidates: Recent Achievements in Medicinal Chemistry, October 26, 2007, Braine-l'Alleud – Brussels, Belgium. 148 Sample International Lectures by Tesfaye Biftu

9. MedChem USA, Oct 9-11, 2007. Boston, Mass.

10. Invited Lecture Series in Diabetes, Inflammation and etc., (2008-2011) Jefferson University, Philadelphia, PA.

11. Invited Lecture, SMR, London, December 2012

12. Invited Lecture Swedish Pharmaceutical Association, Stockholm, 2013

13. Invited lecture, ACS national meeting, September 2013

14. Invited lecture for ACS meeting in Dallas 2013

15. Invited lecture at EFMC, Lisbon, September 6, 2014

ANNEX III: USA Patents

Patents by Inventor Tesfaye Biftu

Tesfaye Biftu has filed for patents to protect the following inventions. This listing includes patent applications that are pending as well as patents that have already been granted by the United States Patent and Trademark Office (USPTO).

Dr. Tesfaye Biftu has been granted patent protection from Justia. Justia provides a browsable database for intellectual property including, trademarks, patents, copyrights and trade secrets; among other legal guides.

Each patent has been hyperlinked to be viewed on Justia.

- **Chromane monobactam compounds for the treatment of bacterial infections**

Patent number: 11433055

Abstract: The present invention relates to monobactam compounds of Formula I: and pharmaceutically acceptable salts thereof. The present invention also relates to compositions which comprise a monobactam compound of the invention or a pharmaceutically acceptable salt thereof, and a pharmaceutically acceptable carrier. The invention further relates to methods for treating a bacterial infection comprising administering to the patient a therapeutically effective amount of a compound of the invention, either alone or in combination with a therapeutically effective amount of a second beta-lactam antibiotic.

Type: Grant

Filed: September 27, 2018

Date of Patent: September 6, 2022

Assignee: Merck Sharp & Dohme LLC

Inventors: Tesfaye Biftu, Xianhai Huang, Weiguo Liu, Weidong Pan, Min Park, Alexander Pasternak, Wanying Sun, Haifeng Tang, Yi Zang

- **Biaryl monobactam compounds and methods of use thereof for the treatment of bacterial infections**

Patent number: 11230543

Abstract: The present invention relates to biaryl monobactam compounds of Formula I: and pharmaceutically acceptable salts thereof, wherein X, Y, Z, A1, Q, A2, M, W, RX and Rz are as defined herein. The present invention also relates to compositions which comprise a biaryl monobactam compound of the invention or a pharmaceutically acceptable salt thereof, and a pharmaceutically acceptable carrier. The invention further relates to methods for treating a bacterial infection comprising administering to the patient a therapeutically effective amount of a compound of the invention, either alone or in combination with a therapeutically effective amount of a second beta-lactam antibiotic.

Type: Grant

Filed: June 25, 2020

Date of Patent: January 25, 2022

Assignee: Merck Sharp & Dohme Corp.

Inventors: Haifeng Tang, Weiguo Liu, Fa-Xiang Ding, Wanying Sun, Yi Zang, Weidong Pan, Anthony Ogawa, Linda Brockunier, Xianhai Huang, Hongwu Wang, Rudrajit Mal, Tesfaye Biftu, Min Park, Yan Guo, Jinlong Jiang, Helen Y. Chen, Christopher W. Plummer

- **BIARYL MONOBACTAM COMPOUNDS AND METHODS OF USE THEREOF FOR THE TREATMENT OF BACTERIAL INFECTIONS**

Publication number: 20200361928

Abstract: The present invention relates to biaryl monobactam compounds of Formula I and pharmaceutically acceptable salts thereof, wherein X, Y, Z, A1, Q, A2, M, W, RX and Rz are as defined herein. The present invention also relates to compositions which comprise a biaryl monobactam compound of the invention or a pharmaceutically acceptable salt thereof, and a pharmaceutically acceptable carrier. The invention further relates to methods for treating a bacterial infection comprising administering to the patient a therapeutically effective amount of a compound of the invention, either alone or in combination with a therapeutically effective amount of a second beta-lactam antibiotic.

Type: Application

Filed: June 25, 2020

Publication date: November 19, 2020

Applicant: Merck Sharp & Dohme Corp.

Inventors: Haifeng Tang, Weiguo Liu, Fa-Xiang Ding, Wanying Sun, Yi Zang, Weidong Pan, Anthony Ogawa, Linda Brockunier, Xianhai Huang, Hongwu Wang, Rudrajit Mal, Tesfaye Biftu, Min Park, Yan Guo, Jinlong Jiang, Helen Y. Chen, Christopher W. Plummer

- **CHROMANE MONOBACTAM COMPOUNDS FOR THE TREATMENT OF BACTERIAL INFECTIONS**

Publication number: 20200297702

Abstract: The present invention relates to monobactam compounds of Formula (I) and pharmaceutically acceptable salts thereof. The present invention also relates to compositions which comprise a monobactam compound of the invention or a pharmaceutically acceptable salt thereof, and a pharmaceutically acceptable carrier. The invention further relates to methods for treating a bacterial infection comprising administering to the patient a therapeutically effective amount of a compound of the invention, either alone or in combination with a therapeutically effective amount of a second beta-lactam antibiotic.

Type: Application

Filed: September 27, 2018

Publication date: September 24, 2020

Applicant: Merck Sharp & Dohme Corp.

Inventors: Tesfaye Biftu, Xianhai Huang, Weiguo Liu, Weidong Pan, Min Park, Alexander Pasternak, Wanying Sun, Haifeng Tang, Yi Zang

- **Antidiabetic tricyclic compounds**

Patent number: 10519115

Abstract: Novel compounds of the structural formula (I), and the pharmaceutically acceptable salts thereof, are agonists of G-protein coupled receptor 40 (GPR40) and may be useful in the treatment, prevention and suppression of diseases mediated by the G-protein-coupled receptor 40. The compounds of the present invention may be useful in the treatment of Type 2 diabetes mellitus, and of conditions that are often associated with this disease, including obesity and lipid disorders, such as mixed or diabetic dyslipidemia, hyperlipidemia, hypercholesterolemia, and hypertriglyceridemia.

Type: Grant

Filed: November 10, 2014

Date of Patent: December 31, 2019

Assignee: Merck Sharp & Dohme Corp.

Inventors: Tesfaye Biftu, Purakkattle Biju, Steven L. Colletti, Qun Dang, Pawan Dhondi, Candido Gude, Hubert Josien, Nam Fung Kar, Anilkumar G. Nair, Ravi P. Nargund, De-Yi Yang, Cheng Zhu

- **<u>Tricyclic compounds as inhibitors of mutant IDH enzymes</u>**

Patent number: 10442819

Abstract: The present invention is directed to tricyclic compounds of formula (I) which are inhibitors of one or more mutant IDH enzymes: (I). The present invention is also directed to uses of the tricyclic compounds described herein in the potential treatment or prevention of cancers in which one or more mutant IDH enzymes are involved. The present invention is also directed to compositions comprising these compounds. The present invention is also directed to uses of these compositions in the potential prevention or treatment of such cancers.

Type: Grant

Filed: December 1, 2015

Date of Patent: October 15, 2019

Assignee: Merck Sharp & Dohme Corp.

Inventors: Christian Fischer, Stephane L. Bogen, Matthew L. Childers, Francesc Xavier Fradera Llinas, J. Michael Ellis, Sara Esposite, Qingmei Hong, Chunhui Huang, Alexander J. Kim, John W. Lampe, Michelle R. Machacek, Daniel R. McMasters, Ryan D. Otte, Dann L. Parker, Jr., Michael Reutershan, Nunzio Sciammetta, Pengcheng P. Shao, David L. Sloman, Feroze Ujjainwalla, Catherine White, Zhicai Wu, Yang Yu, Kake Zhao, Craig Gibeau, Tesfaye Biftu, Purakkattle Biju, Lei Chen, Joshua Close, Peter H. Fuller, Xianhai Huang, Min K. Park, Valdimir Simov, David J. Witter, Hongjun Zhang

- **Tricyclic compounds as inhibitors of mutant IDH enzymes**

Patent number: 10399972

Abstract: The present invention is directed to tricyclic compounds of formula (I), (Ia) or (Ib) which are inhibitors of one or more mutant IDH enzymes. The present invention is also directed to uses of these tricyclic compounds in the potential treatment or prevention of cancers in which one or more mutant IDH enzymes are involved. The present invention is also directed to compositions comprising these compounds. The present invention is also directed to uses of these compositions in the potential prevention or treatment of such cancers.

Type: Grant

Filed: October 25, 2016

Date of Patent: September 3, 2019

Assignee: Merck Sharp & Dohme Corp.

Inventors: David J. Witter, Tesfaye Biftu, Purakkattle Biju, Stephane L. Bogen, Qingmei Hong, Chunhui Huang, Xianhai Huang, Bing Li, Min K. Park, David L. Sloman

- **BIARYL MONOBACTAM COMPOUNDS AND METHODS OF USE THEREOF FOR THE TREATMENT OF BACTERIAL INFECTIONS**

Publication number: 20180339983

Abstract: The present invention relates to biaryl monobactam compounds of Formula I: and pharmaceutically acceptable salts thereof, wherein X, Y, Z, A1, Q, M, W, RX and Rz are as defined herein. The present invention also relates to compositions which comprise a biaryl monobactam compound of the invention or a pharmaceutically acceptable salt thereof, and a pharmaceutically acceptable carrier. The invention further relates to methods for treating a bacterial infection comprising administering to the patient a therapeutically effective amount of a compound of the invention, either alone or in combination with a therapeutically effective amount of a second beta-lactam antibiotic.

Type: Application

Filed: December 12, 2016

Publication date: November 29, 2018

Applicant: Merck Sharp & Dohme Corp.

Inventors: Haifeng Tang, Weiguo Liu, Fa-Xiang Ding, Wanying Sun, Yi Zang, Weidong Pan, Anthony Ogawa, Linda Brockunier, Xianhai Huang, Hongwu Wang, Rudrajit Mal, Tesfaye Biftu, Min Park, Yan Guo, Jinlong Jiang, Helen Y. Chen, Christopher W. Plummer

- **NOVEL TRICYCLIC COMPOUNDS AS INHIBITORS OF MUTANT IDH ENZYMES**

Publication number: 20180305352

Abstract: The present invention is directed to tricyclic compounds of formula (I), (Ia) or (Ib) which are inhibitors of one or more mutant IDH enzymes. The present invention is also directed to uses of these tricyclic compounds in the potential treatment or prevention of cancers in which one or more mutant IDH enzymes are involved. The present invention is also directed to compositions comprising these compounds. The present invention is also directed to uses of these compositions in the potential prevention or treatment of such cancers.

Type: Application

Filed: October 25, 2016

Publication date: October 25, 2018

Applicant: Merck Sharp & Dohme Corp.

Inventors: David J. Witter, Tesfaye Biftu, Purakkattle Biju, Stephane L. Bogen, Qingmei Hong, Chunhui Huang, Xianhai Huang, Bing Li, Min K. Park, David L. Sloman

- **Antidiabetic tricyclic compounds**

Patent number: 10000454

Abstract: Novel compounds of the structural formula (I), and the pharmaceutically acceptable salts thereof, are agonists of G-protein coupled receptor 40 (GPR40) and may be useful in the treatment, prevention and suppression of diseases mediated by the G-protein-coupled receptor 40. The compounds of the present invention may be useful in the treatment of Type 2 diabetes mellitus, and of conditions that are often associated with this disease, including obesity and lipid disorders, such as mixed or diabetic dyslipidemia, hyperlipidemia, hypercholesterolemia, and hypertriglyceridemia.

Type: Grant

Filed: May 19, 2015

Date of Patent: June 19, 2018

Assignee: Merck Sharp & Dohme

Inventors: Tesfaye Biftu, Purakkattle Biju, Timothy A. Blizzard, Zhengxia Chen, Matthew J. Clements, Mingxiang Cui, Jessica L. Frie, William K. Hagmann, Bin Hu, Hubert Josien, Anilkumar G. Nair, Christopher W. Plummer, Cheng Zhu

- **Antidiabetic tricyclic compounds**

Patent number: 9932311

Abstract: Novel compounds of the structural formula (I), and the pharmaceutically acceptable salts thereof, are agonists of G-protein coupled receptor 40 (GPR40) and may be useful in the treatment, prevention and suppression of diseases mediated by the G-protein-coupled receptor 40. The compounds of the present invention may be useful in the treatment of Type 2 diabetes mellitus, and of conditions that are often associated with this disease, including obesity and lipid disorders, such as mixed or diabetic dyslipidemia, hyperlipidemia, hypercholesterolemia, and hypertriglyceridemia.

Type: Grant

Filed: September 30, 2014

Date of Patent: April 3, 2018

Assignee: Merck Sharp & Dohme Corp.

Inventors: Tesfaye Biftu, Purakkattle Biju, Steven L. Colletti, Mingxiang Cui, William K Hagmann, Bin Hu, Hubert Josien, Nam Fung Kar, Anilkumar Nair, Ravi Nargund, Donald M. Sperbeck, Cheng Zhu

- **Azabenzimidazole tetrahydrofuran derivatives**

Patent number: 9868733

Abstract: Novel compounds of the structural formula (I) are activators of AMP-protein kinase and may be useful in the treatment, prevention and suppression of diseases mediated by the AMPK-activated protein kinase. The compounds of the present invention may be useful in the treatment of Type 2 diabetes, hyperglycemia, metabolic syndrome, obesity, hypercholesterolemia, and hypertension.

Type: Grant

Filed: August 19, 2013

Date of Patent: January 16, 2018

Assignee: Merck Sharp & Dohme Corp.

Inventors: James M. Apgar, Tesfaye Biftu, Ping Chen, Danqing Feng, Jacqueline D. Hicks, Ahmet Kekec, Kenneth J. Leavitt, Bing Li, Iyassu Sebhat, Xiaoxia Qian, Lan Wei, Robert R. Wilkening, Zhicai Wu, Ashok Arasappan

- **ANTIDIABETIC TRICYCLIC COMPOUNDS**

Publication number: 20170081287

Abstract: Novel compounds of the structural formula (I), and the pharmaceutically acceptable salts thereof, are agonists of G-protein coupled receptor 40 (GPR40) and may be useful in the treatment, prevention and suppression of diseases mediated by the G-protein-coupled receptor 40. The compounds of the present invention may be useful in the treatment of Type 2 diabetes mellitus, and of conditions that are often associated with this disease, including obesity and lipid disorders, such as mixed or diabetic dyslipidemia, hyperlipidemia, hypercholesterolemia, and hypertriglyceridemia.

Type: Application

Filed: May 19, 2015

Publication date: March 23, 2017

Inventors: Tesfaye Biftu, Purakkattle Biju, Timothy A. Blizzard, Zhengxia Chen, Matthew J. Clements, Mingxiang Cui, Jessica L. Frie, William K. Hagmann, Bin Hu, Hubert Josien, Anilkumar G. Nair, Christopher W. Plummer, Cheng Zhu

- **Benzimidazole hexahydrofuro[3,2-b]furan derivatives**

Patent number: 9556193

Abstract: The novel benzimidazole hexahydrofuro[3,2-B]furan derivatives of the present invention are activators of AMP-protein kinase and may be useful in the treatment, prevention and suppression of diseases mediated by the AMPK-activated protein kinase. The compounds of the present invention may be useful in the treatment of Type 2 diabetes, hyperglycemia, metabolic syndrome, obesity, hypercholesterolemia, and hypertension.

Type: Grant

Filed: August 16, 2013

Date of Patent: January 31, 2017

Assignee: Merck Shapr & Dohme Corp.

Inventors: James M. Apgar, Ashok Arasappan, Tesfaye Biftu, Ping Chen, Danqing Feng, Erin Guidry, Jacqueline Hicks, Ahmet Kekec, Kenneth J. Leavitt, Bing Li, Iyassu Sebhat, Xiaoxia Qian, Lan Wei, Robert R. Wilkening, Zhicai Wu

- **Benzimidazole tetrahydrofuran derivatives**

Patent number: 9540364

Abstract: Novel compounds of the structural formula (I) are activators of AMP-protein kinase and may be useful in the treatment, prevention and suppression of diseases mediated by the AMPK-activated protein kinase. The compounds of the present invention may be useful in the treatment of Type 2 diabetes, hyperglycemia, metabolic syndrome, obesity, hypercholesterolemia, and hypertension.

Type: Grant

Filed: August 15, 2013

Date of Patent: January 10, 2017

Assignee: Merck Sharp & Dohme Corp.

Inventors: James M. Apgar, Tesfaye Biftu, Ping Chen, Danqing Feng, Jacqueline D. Hicks, Ahmet Kekec, Kenneth J. Leavitt, Bing Li, Iyassu Sebhat, Xiaoxia Qian, Lan Wei, Robert R. Wilkening, Zhicai Wu

- **<u>Benzimidazole tetrahydropyran derivatives</u>**

Patent number: 9527839

Abstract: Novel compounds described herein are activators of AMP-protein kinase and may be useful in the treatment, prevention and suppression of diseases mediated by the AMPKactivated protein kinase. The compounds of the present invention may be useful in the treatment of Type 2 diabetes, hyperglycemia, metabolic syndrome, obesity, hypercholesterolemia, and hypertension.

Type: Grant

Filed: August 15, 2013

Date of Patent: December 27, 2016

Assignee: Merck Sharp & Dohme Corp.

Inventors: James M. Apgar, Tesfaye Biftu, Ping Chen, Danqing Feng, Jacqueline D. Hicks, Ahmet Kekec, Kenneth J. Leavitt, Bing Li, Iyassu Sebhat, Xiaoxia Qian, Lan Wei, Robert R. Wilkening, Zhicai Wu

- **Thrombin inhibitors**

Patent number: 9469608

Abstract: Compounds of the invention, which may be useful in inhibiting thrombin and associated thrombotic occlusions, have the following structure: or a pharmaceutically acceptable salt thereof, wherein m is 0 or 1; R is a heterocycle, —(CR8R9)1-2NH2, or —(CR8R9)1-2OH, wherein R8 and R9, each time in which they occur, are independently H, C1-6alkyl, —CH2F, —CHF2, CF3 or —CH2OH; W is a) —CHR1R2, where R1 is —C(CH3)3, and R2 is —(CH2)1-2OH, b) a 5- or 6-membered unsubstituted or substituted heterocycle having 1 or 2 heteroatoms selected from N and O, wherein substituted heterocycle is substituted with R3, c) a 9- or 10-membered unsubstituted or substituted heterocycle having 1 or 2 heteroatoms selected from N, O and S, wherein substituted heterocycle is mono-substituted with R3, or substituted with R3 and R4, or d) a 3-, 4-, or 5-membered carbocyclic ring which is unsubstituted, mono-substituted with R3, di-substituted with R3 and R4, or tri-substituted with R3, R4 and R5; R3 is —CF3, —COOH, —COOR7, —C(O)R6, —CH(OH)R6,

Type: Grant

Filed: November 15, 2013

Date of Patent: October 18, 2016

Assignee: Merck Sharp & Dohme Corp.

Inventors: Harry Chobanian, Tesfaye Biftu, Barbara Pio, Zhicai Wu

- **Iminothiadiazine dioxides containing a thioamide, amidine, or amide oxime group as BACE inhibitors, compositions, and their use**

Patent number: 9447085

Abstract: In its many embodiments, the present invention provides certain C2-ring-substituted iminothiadiazine compounds, or a tautomers thereof, and pharmaceutically acceptable salts of said compounds and said tautomers. The novel compounds of the invention are as BACE inhibitors and/or for the treatment and prevention of various pathologies related thereto. Pharmaceutical compositions comprising one or more such compounds (alone and in combination with one or more other active agents), and methods for their preparation and use, including for the possible treatment of Alzheimer's disease, are also disclosed.

Type: Grant

Filed: December 9, 2013

Date of Patent: September 20, 2016

Assignee: Merck Sharp & Dohme Corp.

Inventors: Jared N. Cumming, Jack D. Scott, Tesfaye Biftu

- **ANTIDIABETIC TRICYCLIC COMPOUNDS**

Publication number: 20160257652

Abstract: Novel compounds of the structural formula (I), and the pharmaceutically acceptable salts thereof, are agonists of G-protein coupled receptor 40 (GPR40) and may be useful in the treatment, prevention and suppression of diseases mediated by the G-protein-coupled receptor 40. The compounds of the present invention may be useful in the treatment of Type 2 diabetes mellitus, and of conditions that are often associated with this disease, including obesity and lipid disorders, such as mixed or diabetic dyslipidemia, hyperlipidemia, hypercholesterolemia, and hypertriglyceridemia.

Type: Application

Filed: November 10, 2014

Publication date: September 8, 2016

Inventors: Tesfaye Biftu, Purakkattle Biju, Steven L. Colletti, Qun Dang, Pawan Dhondi, Candido Gude, Hubert Josien, Nam Fung Kar, Anilkumar G. Nair, Ravi P. Nargund, De-Yi Yang, Cheng Zhu

- **Aminotetrahydropyrans as dipeptidyl peptidase-IV inhibitors for the treatment or prevention of diabetes**

Patent number: 9403790

Abstract: The present invention is directed to novel substituted amino tetrahydropyran of structural formula I which are inhibitors of the dipeptidyl peptidase-IV enzyme and which are useful in the treatment or prevention of diseases in which the dipeptidyl peptidase-IV enzyme is involved, such as diabetes and particularly Type 2 diabetes. The invention is also directed to pharmaceutical compositions comprising these compounds and the use of these compounds and compositions in the prevention or treatment of such diseases in which the dipeptidyl peptidase-IV enzyme is involved.

Type: Grant

Filed: January 26, 2016

Date of Patent: August 2, 2016

Assignee: Merck Sharp & Dohme Corp.

Inventors: Tesfaye Biftu, Ann E. Weber, Ping Chen

- **ANTIDIABETIC TRICYCLIC COMPOUNDS**

Publication number: 20160207887

Abstract: Novel compounds of the structural formula (I), and the pharmaceutically acceptable salts thereof, are agonists of G-protein coupled receptor 40 (GPR40) and may be useful in the treatment, prevention and suppression of diseases mediated by the G-protein-coupled receptor 40. The compounds of the present invention may be useful in the treatment of Type 2 diabetes mellitus, and of conditions that are often associated with this disease, including obesity and lipid disorders, such as mixed or diabetic dyslipidemia, hyperlipidemia, hypercholesterolemia, and hypertriglyceridemia.

Type: Application

Filed: September 30, 2014

Publication date: July 21, 2016

Inventors: Tesfaye Biftu, Purakkattle Biju, Steven L. Colletti, Mingxiang Cui, William K. Hagmann, Bin Hu, Hubert Josien, Nam Fung Kar, Anilkumar Nair, Ravi Nargund, Donald M. Sperbeck, Cheng Zhu

- **Azabenzimidazole tetrahydropyran derivatives**

Patent number: 9382243

Abstract: Novel compounds of the structural formula (I) are activators of AMP-protein kinase and may be useful in the treatment, prevention and suppression of diseases mediated by the AMPK activated protein kinase. The compounds of the present invention may be useful in the treatment of Type 2 diabetes, hyperglycemia, metabolic syndrome, obesity, hypercholesterolemia, and hypertension.

Type: Grant

Filed: August 16, 2013

Date of Patent: July 5, 2016

Assignee: Merck Sharp & Dohme Corp.

Inventors: James M. Apgar, Tesfaye Biftu, Ping Chen, Danqing Feng, Jacqueline D. Hicks, Ahmet Kekec, Kenneth J. Leavitt, Bing Li, Iyassu Sebhat, Xiaoxia Qian, Lan Wei, Robert R. Wilkening, Zhicai Wu

- **AMINOTETRAHYDROPYRANS AS DIPEPTIDYL PEPTIDASE-IV INHIBITORS FOR THE TREATMENT OR PREVENTION OF DIABETES**

Publication number: 20160137622

Abstract: The present invention is directed to novel substituted amino tetrahydropyran of structural formula I which are inhibitors of the dipeptidyl peptidase-IV enzyme and which are useful in the treatment or prevention of diseases in which the dipeptidyl peptidase-IV enzyme is involved, such as diabetes and particularly Type 2 diabetes. The invention is also directed to pharmaceutical compositions comprising these compounds and the use of these compounds and compositions in the prevention or treatment of such diseases in which the dipeptidyl peptidase-IV enzyme is involved.

Type: Application

Filed: January 26, 2016

Publication date: May 19, 2016

Inventors: Tesfaye Biftu, Ann E. Weber

- **Preparation and use of bicyclic himbacine derivatives as PAR-1 receptor antagonists**

Patent number: 9340530

Abstract: The present invention relates to bicyclic himbacine derivatives of the formula or a pharmaceutically acceptable salt thereof, wherein: X is —O—, —N(R), —C(R8)(R9) or —C(O)—; and Y is —O—, —N(R), —C(R8)(R9) or —C(O)— and the remaining variables are described herein. The compounds of the invention are effective inhibitors of the PAR-1 receptor. The inventive compounds may be used for the treatment or prophylaxis of disease states such as ACS, secondary prevention of myocardial infarction or stroke, or PAD.

Type: Grant

Filed: February 27, 2013

Date of Patent: May 17, 2016

Assignee: Merck Sharp & Dohme Corp.

Inventors: Mihir Mandal, Timothy A. Blizzard, Helen Chen, Harry Chobanian, Yan Guo, Barbara Pio, Zhicai Wu, Tesfaye Biftu, William J. Greenlee, Johnny Zhaoning Zhu

- **Treating diabetes with dipeptidyl peptidase-IV inhibitors**

Patent number: 9315508

Abstract: The present invention is directed to novel substituted dihydropyrrole pyrazoles of structural Formula I which are inhibitors of the dipeptidyl peptidase-AN enzyme and which are useful in the treatment or prevention of diseases in which the dipeptidyl peptidase-IV enzyme is involved, such as diabetes and particularly Type 2 diabetes. The invention is also directed to pharmaceutical compositions comprising these compounds and the use of these compounds and compositions in the prevention or treatment of such diseases in which the dipeptidyl peptidase IV enzyme is involved.

Type: Grant

Filed: July 18, 2013

Date of Patent: April 19, 2016

Assignee: Merck sharp & Dohme Corp.

Inventor: Tesfaye Biftu

- **Spirolactam CGRP receptor antagonists**

Patent number: 9296750

Abstract: The present invention is directed to spirolactam analogs which are antagonists of CGRP receptors and useful in the treatment or prevention of diseases in which CGRP is involved, such as migraine. The invention is also directed to pharmaceutical compositions comprising these compounds and the use of these compounds and compositions in the prevention or treatment of such diseases in which CGRP is involved.

Type: Grant

Filed: May 3, 2013

Date of Patent: March 29, 2016

Assignee: Merck Sharp & Dohme Corp.

Inventors: Ian M. Bell, Mark Fraley, Tesfaye Biftu, Cheng Zhu, Anilkumar Nair

- **Azabenzimidazole hexahydrofuro[3,2-b]furan derivatives**

Patent number: 9290517

Abstract: Novel compounds of the structural formula (I) are activators of AMP-protein kinase and may be useful in the treatment, prevention and suppression of diseases mediated by the AMPK activated protein kinase. The compounds of the present invention may be useful in the treatment of Type 2 diabetes, hyperglycemia, metabolic syndrome, obesity, hypercholesterolemia, and hypertension.

Type: Grant

Filed: August 19, 2013

Date of Patent: March 22, 2016

Assignee: Merck Sharp & Dohme Corp.

Inventors: James M. Apgar, Ashok Arasappan, Tesfaye Biftu, Ping Chen, Danqing Feng, Erin Guidry, Jacqueline D. Hicks, Ahmet Kekec, Kenneth J. Leavitt, Bing Li, Troy McCracken, Iyassu Sebhat, Xiaoxia Qian, Lan Wei, Robert R. Wilkening, Zhicai Wu

- **Aminotetrahydropyrans as dipeptidyl peptidase-IV inhibitors for the treatment of diabetes**

Patent number: 9278976

Abstract: The present invention is directed to novel substituted amino tetrahydropyran of structural formula I which are inhibitors of the dipeptidyl peptidase-IV enzyme and which are useful in the treatment or prevention of diseases in which the dipeptidyl peptidase-IV enzyme is involved, such as diabetes and particularly Type 2 diabetes. The invention is also directed to pharmaceutical compositions comprising these compounds and the use of these compounds and compositions in the prevention or treatment of such diseases in which the dipeptidyl peptidase-IV enzyme is involved.

Type: Grant

Filed: August 13, 2015

Date of Patent: March 8, 2016

Assignee: Merck Sharp & Dohme Corp.

Inventors: Tesfaye Biftu, Ann E. Weber

- **Pyridine CGRP receptor antagonists**

Patent number: 9227973

Abstract: The present invention is directed to pyridine derivatives which are antagonists of CGRP receptors and useful in the treatment or prevention of diseases in which CGRP is involved, such as migraine. The invention is also directed to pharmaceutical compositions comprising these compounds and the use of these compounds and compositions in the prevention or treatment of such diseases in which CGRP is involved.

Type: Grant

Filed: May 3, 2013

Date of Patent: January 5, 2016

Assignee: Merck Sharp & Dohme Corp.

Inventors: Ian M. Bell, Mark Fraley, Tesfaye Biftu, Cheng Zhu, Anilkumar Nair

- **<u>Aliphatic spirolactam CGRP receptor antagonists</u>**

Patent number: 9227972

Abstract: The present invention is directed to aliphatic spirolactam derivatives which are antagonists of CGRP receptors and useful in the treatment or prevention of diseases in which CGRP is involved, such as migraine. The invention is also directed to pharmaceutical\compositions comprising these compounds and the use of these compounds and compositions in the prevention or treatment of such diseases in which CGRP is involved.

Type: Grant

Filed: May 3, 2013

Date of Patent: January 5, 2016

Assignee: Merck Sharp & Dohme Corp.

Inventors: Ian M. Bell, Mark Fraley, Tesfaye Biftu, Cheng Zhu, Anilkumar Nair, Helen Mitchell

- **IMINOTHIADIAZINE DIOXIDES CONTAINING A THIOAMIDE, AMIDINE, OR AMIDE OXIME GROUP AS BACE INHIBITORS, COMPOSITIONS, AND THEIR USE**

Publication number: 20150353516

Abstract: In its many embodiments, the present invention provides certain C2-ring-substituted iminothiadiazine compounds, or a tautomers thereof, and pharmaceutically acceptable salts of said compounds and said tautomers. The novel compounds of the invention are as BACE inhibitors and/or for the treatment and prevention of various pathologies related thereto. Pharmaceutical compositions comprising one or more such compounds (alone and in combination with one or more other active agents), and methods for their preparation and use, including for the possible treatment of Alzheimer's disease, are also disclosed.

Type: Application

Filed: December 9, 2013

Publication date: December 10, 2015

Inventors: Jared N. Cumming, Jack D. Scott, Tesfaye Biftu

- **AMINOTETRAHYDROPYRANS AS DIPEPTIDYL PEPTIDASE-IV INHIBITORS FOR THE TREATMENT OF DIABETES**

Publication number: 20150344487

Abstract: The present invention is directed to novel substituted amino tetrahydropyran of structural formula I which are inhibitors of the dipeptidyl peptidase-IV enzyme and which are useful in the treatment or prevention of diseases in which the dipeptidyl peptidase-IV enzyme is involved, such as diabetes and particularly Type 2 diabetes. The invention is also directed to pharmaceutical compositions comprising these compounds and the use of these compounds and compositions in the prevention or treatment of such diseases in which the dipeptidyl peptidase-IV enzyme is involved.

Type: Application

Filed: August 13, 2015

Publication date: December 3, 2015

Inventors: Tesfaye Biftu, Ann E. Weber

- **Crystalline forms of a dipeptidyl peptidase-IV inhibitors**

Patent number: 9181262

Abstract: Novel crystalline forms of (2R,3S,5R)-2-(2,5-Difluorophenyl)-5-[2-(methylsulfonyl)-2,6-dihydropyrrolo[3,4-c]pyrazol-5(4H)-yl]tetrahydro-2H-pyran-3-amine are potent inhibitors of dipeptidyl peptidase-IV and are useful for the treatment of non-insulin dependent (Type 2) diabetes mellitus. The invention also relates to pharmaceutical compositions containing these novel forms, processes to prepare these forms and their pharmaceutical compositions as well as uses thereof for the treatment of Type 2 diabetes.

Type: Grant

Filed: October 6, 2014

Date of Patent: November 10, 2015

Assignees: Merck Sharp & Dohme Corp, Merck Sharp & Dohme Ltd.

Inventors: Itzia Z. Arroyo, Davida Krueger, Ping Chen, Aaron J. Moment, Tesfaye Biftu, Faye Sheen, Yanfeng Zhang

- **Thrombin Inhibitors**

Publication number: 20150315141

Abstract: Compounds of the invention, which may be useful in inhibiting thrombin and associated thrombotic occlusions, have the following structure: or a pharmaceutically acceptable salt thereof, wherein m is 0 or 1; R is a heterocycle, —(CR8R9)1-2NH2, or —(CR8R9)1-2OH, wherein R8 and R9, each time in which they occur, are independently H, C1-6 alkyl, —CH2F, —CHF2, CF3 or —CH2OH; W is a) —CHR1R2, where R1 is —C(CH3)3, and R2 is —(CH2)1-2OH, b) a 5- or 6-membered unsubstituted or substituted heterocycle having 1 or 2 heteroatoms selected from N and O, wherein substituted heterocycle is substituted with R3, c) a 9- or 10-membered unsubstituted or substituted heterocycle having 1 or 2 heteroatoms selected from N, O and S, wherein substituted heterocycle is mono-substituted with R3, or disubstituted with R3 and R4, or d) a 3-, 4-, or 5-membered carbocyclic ring which is unsubstituted, mono-substituted with R3, di-substituted with R3 and R4, or tri-substituted with R3, R4 and R5; R3 is —CF3, —COOH, —COOR7, —C(O)R6, —CH

Type: Application

Filed: November 15, 2013

Publication date: November 5, 2015

Applicant: Merck Sharp & Dohme Corp.

Inventors: Harry Chobanian, Tesfaye Biftu, Barbara Pio, Zhicai Wu

- **<u>Treating diabetes with dipeptidyl peptidase-IV inhibitors</u>**

Patent number: 9156848

Abstract: The present invention is directed to novel substituted dihydropyrrolopyrazoles of structural Formula I which are inhibitors of the dipeptidyl peptidase-N enzyme and which are useful in the treatment or prevention of diseases in which the dipeptidyl peptidase-IV enzyme is involved, such as diabetes and particularly Type 2 diabetes. The invention is also directed to pharmaceutical compositions comprising these compounds and the use of these compounds and compositions in the prevention or treatment of such diseases in which the dipeptidyl peptidase IV enzyme is involved.

Type: Grant

Filed: July 18, 2013

Date of Patent: October 13, 2015

Assignee: Merck Sharp & Dohme Corp.

Inventors: Tesfaye Biftu, Tanweer A. Khan

- **NOVEL AZABENZIMIDAZOLE HEXAHYDROFURO [E,2-B]FURAN DERIVATIVES**

Publication number: 20150284411

Abstract: Novel compounds of the structural formula (I) are activators of AMP-protein kinase and may be useful in the treatment, prevention and suppression of diseases mediated by the AMPK activated protein kinase. The compounds of the present invention may be useful in the treatment of Type 2 diabetes, hyperglycemia, metabolic syndrome, obesity, hypercholesterolemia, and hypertension.

Type: Application

Filed: August 19, 2013

Publication date: October 8, 2015

Inventors: James M. Apgar, Ashok Arasappan, Tesfaye Biftu, Ping Chen, Danqing Feng, Erin Guidry, Jacqueline D. Hicks, Ahmet Kekec, Kenneth J. Leavitt, Bing Li, Troy McCracken, Iyassu Sebhat, Xiaoxia Qian, Lan Wei, Robert R. Wilkening, Zhicai Wu

- **Aminotetrahydropyrans as dipeptidyl peptidase-IV inhibitors for the treatment of diabetes**

Patent number: 9138426

Abstract: The present invention is directed to novel substituted aminotetrahydropyrans of structural formula I which are inhibitors of the

dipeptidyl peptidase-IV enzyme and which are useful in the treatment or prevention of diseases in which the dipeptidyl peptidase-IV enzyme is involved, such as diabetes and particularly Type 2 diabetes. The invention is also directed to pharmaceutical compositions comprising these compounds and the use of these compounds and compositions in the prevention or treatment of such diseases in which the dipeptidyl peptidase-IV enzyme is involved.

Type: Grant

Filed: January 7, 2015

Date of Patent: September 22, 2015

Assignee: Merck Sharp & Dohme Corp.

Inventors: Tesfaye Biftu, Ann E. Weber

- **Thrombin inhibitors**

Patent number: 9133147

Abstract: Compounds of the invention are useful in inhibiting thrombin and associated thrombotic occlusions having the following structure: or a pharmaceutically acceptable salt thereof, wherein Q is CH2, NR4, O, S, S(O) or S(O2), wherein R4 is H, C1-6 alkyl, aryl, or C3-8 cycloalkyl; R1 is a heterocycle or —(CR5R6)1-2NH2, wherein R5 and R6, each time in which they occur, are independently H, C1-6 alkyl, —CH2F, —CHF2, CF3 or —CH2OH; R2 is OH, NH2 or NHSO2CH3; R3 is C1-6 alkyl.

Type: Grant

Filed: March 22, 2013

Date of Patent: September 15, 2015

Assignee: Merck Sharp & Dohme Corp.

Inventors: Timothy Allen Blizzard, Tesfaye Biftu

- **TREATING DIABETES WITH DIPEPTIDYL PEPTIDASE-IV INHIBITORS**

Publication number: 20150225402

Abstract: The present invention is directed to novel substituted dihydropyrrolopyrazoles of structural Formula I which are inhibitors of the dipeptidyl peptidase-N enzyme and which are useful in the treatment or prevention of diseases in which the dipeptidyl peptidase-IV enzyme is involved, such as diabetes and particularly Type 2 diabetes. The invention is also directed to pharmaceutical compositions comprising these compounds and the use of these compounds and compositions in the prevention or treatment of such diseases in which the dipeptidyl peptidase IV enzyme is involved.

Type: Application

Filed: July 18, 2013

Publication date: August 13, 2015

Inventor: Tesfaye Biftu

- **NOVEL BENZIMIDAZOLE TETRAHYDROFURAN DERIVATIVES**

Publication number: 20150218149

Abstract: Novel compounds of the structural formula (I) are activators of AMP-protein kinase and may be useful in the treatment, prevention and suppression of diseases mediated by the AMPK-activated protein kinase. The compounds of the present invention may be useful in the treatment of Type 2 diabetes, hyperglycemia, metabolic syndrome, obesity, hypercholesterolemia, and hypertension.

Type: Application

Filed: August 15, 2013

Publication date: August 6, 2015

Inventors: James M. Apgar, Tesfaye Biftu, Ping Chen, Danqing Feng, Jacqueline D. Hicks, Ahmet Kekec, Kenneth J. Leavitt, Bing Li, Iyassu Sebhat, Xiaoxia Qian, Lan Wei, Robert R. Wilkening, Zhicai Wu

- **NOVEL BENZIMIDAZOLE HEXAHYDROFURO[3,2-B] FURAN DERIVATIVES**

Publication number: 20150218183

Abstract: The novel benzimidazole hexahydrofuro[3,2-B]furan derivatives of the present invention are activators of AMP-protein kinase and may be useful in the treatment, prevention and suppression of diseases mediated by the AMPK-activated protein kinase. The compounds of the present invention may be useful in the treatment of Type 2 diabetes, hyperglycemia, metabolic syndrome, obesity, hypercholesterolemia, and hypertension.

Type: Application

Filed: August 16, 2013

Publication date: August 6, 2015

Inventors: James M. Apgar, Ashok Arasappan, Tesfaye Biftu, Ping Chen, Danqing Feng, Erin Guidry, Jacqueline Hicks, Ahmet Kekec, Kenneth J. Leavitt, Bing Li, Iyassu Sebhat, Xiaoxia Qian, Lan Wei, Robert R. Wilkening, Zhicai Wu

- **NOVEL AZABENZIMIDAZOLE TETRAHYDROPYRAN DERIVATIVES**

Publication number: 20150210685

Abstract: Novel compounds of the structural formula (I) are activators of AMP-protein kinase and may be useful in the treatment, prevention and suppression of diseases mediated by the AMPKactivated protein kinase. The compounds of the present invention may be useful in the treatment of Type 2 diabetes, hyperglycemia, metabolic syndrome, obesity, hypercholesterolemia, and hypertension.

Type: Application

Filed: August 16, 2013

Publication date: July 30, 2015

Inventors: James M. Apgar, Tesfaye Biftu, Ping Chen, Danqing Feng, Jacqueline D. Hicks, Ahmet Kekec, Kenneth J. Leavitt, Bing Li, Iyassu Sebhat, Xiaoxia Qian, Lan Wei, Robert R. Wilkening, Zhicai Wu

- **NOVEL AZABENZIMIDAZOLE TETRAHYDROFURAN DERIVATIVES**

Publication number: 20150203487

Abstract: Novel compounds of the structural formula (I) are activators of AMP-protein kinase and may be useful in the treatment, prevention and suppression of diseases mediated by the AMPK-activated protein kinase. The compounds of the present invention may be useful in the treatment of Type 2 diabetes, hyperglycemia, metabolic syndrome, obesity, hypercholesterolemia, and hypertension.

Type: Application

Filed: August 19, 2013

Publication date: July 23, 2015

Inventors: James M. Apgar, Tesfaye Biftu, Ping Chen, Danqing Feng, Jacqueline D. Hicks, Ahmet Kekec, Kenneth J. Leavitt, Bing Li, Iyassu Sebhat, Xiaoxia Qian, Lan Wei, Robert R. Wilkening, Zhicai Wu, Ashok Arasappan

- **ALIPHATIC SPIROLACTAM CGRP RECEPTOR ANTAGONISTS**

Publication number: 20150203496

Abstract: The present invention is directed to aliphatic spirolactam derivatives which are antagonists of CGRP receptors and useful in the treatment or prevention of diseases in which CGRP is involved, such as migraine. The invention is also directed to pharmaceutical\compositions comprising these compounds and the use of these compounds and compositions in the prevention or treatment of such diseases in which CGRP is involved.

Type: Application

Filed: May 3, 2013

Publication date: July 23, 2015

Inventors: Ian M. Bell, Mark Fraley, Tesfaye Biftu, Cheng Zhu, Anilkumar Nair, Helen Mitchell

- **NOVEL BENZIMIDAZOLE TETRAHYDROPYRAN DERIVATIVES**

Publication number: 20150197516

Abstract: Novel compounds described herein are activators of AMP-protein kinase and may be useful in the treatment, prevention and suppression of diseases mediated by the AMPKactivated protein kinase. The compounds of the present invention may be useful in the treatment of Type 2 diabetes, hyperglycemia, metabolic syndrome, obesity, hypercholesterolemia, and hypertension.

Type: Application

Filed: August 15, 2013

Publication date: July 16, 2015

Inventors: James M. Apgar, Tesfaye Biftu, Ping Chen, Danqing Feng, Jacqueline D. Hicks, Ahmet Kekec, Kenneth J. Leavitt, Bing Li, Iyassu Sebhat, Xiaoxia Qian, Lan Wei, Robert R. Wilkening, Zhicai Wu

- **Dipeptidyl peptidase-IV inhibitors for the treatment or prevention of diabetes**

Patent number: 9073930

Abstract: The present invention is directed to novel substituted dihydropyrrolopyrazoles of structural Formula I which are inhibitors of the

dipeptidyl peptidase-IV enzyme and which are useful in the treatment or prevention of diseases in which the dipeptidyl peptidase-IV enzyme is involved, such as diabetes and particularly Type 2 diabetes. The invention is also directed to pharmaceutical compositions comprising these compounds and the use of these compounds and compositions in the prevention or treatment of such diseases in which the dipeptidyl peptidase-IV enzyme is involved.

Type: Grant

Filed: February 12, 2013

Date of Patent: July 7, 2015

Assignee: Merck Sharp & Dohme

Inventors: Ann E. Weber, Tesfaye Biftu

- **TREATING DIABETES WITH DIPEPTIDYL PEPTIDASE-IV INHIBITORS**

Publication number: 20150175609

Abstract: The present invention is directed to novel substituted dihydropyrrolopyrazoles of structural Formula I which are inhibitors of the dipeptidyl peptidase-N enzyme and which are useful in the treatment or prevention of diseases in which the dipeptidyl peptidase-IV enzyme is involved, such as diabetes and particularly Type 2 diabetes. The invention is also directed to pharmaceutical compositions comprising these compounds and the use of these compounds and compositions in the prevention or treatment of such diseases in which the dipeptidyl peptidase IV enzyme is involved.

Type: Application

Filed: July 18, 2013

Publication date: June 25, 2015

Inventors: Tesfaye Biftu, Tanweer A. Khan

- **AMINOTETRAHYDROPYRANS AS DIPEPTIDYL PEPTIDASE-IV INHIBITORS FOR THE TREATMENT OF DIABETES**

Publication number: 20150126443

Abstract: The present invention is directed to novel substituted aminotetrahydropyrans of structural formula I which are inhibitors of the dipeptidyl peptidase-IV enzyme and which are useful in the treatment or prevention of diseases in which the dipeptidyl peptidase-IV enzyme is involved, such as diabetes and particularly Type 2 diabetes. The invention is also directed to pharmaceutical compositions comprising these compounds and the use of these compounds and compositions in the prevention or treatment of such diseases in which the dipeptidyl peptidase-IV enzyme is involved.

Type: Application

Filed: January 7, 2015

Publication date: May 7, 2015

Inventors: Tesfaye Biftu, Ann E. Weber

- **SPIROLACTAM CGRP RECEPTOR ANTAGONISTS**

Publication number: 20150111914

Abstract: The present invention is directed to spirolactam analogues which are antagonists of CGRP receptors and useful in the treatment or prevention of diseases in which CGRP is involved, such as migraine. The invention is also directed to pharmaceutical compositions comprising these compounds and the use of these compounds and compositions in the prevention or treatment of such diseases in which CGRP is involved.

Type: Application

Filed: May 3, 2013

Publication date: April 23, 2015

Inventors: Ian M. Bell, Mark Fraley, Tesfaye Biftu, Cheng Zhu, Anilkumar Nair

- **NOVEL CRYSTALLINE FORMS OF A DIPEPTIDYL PEPTIDASE-IV INHIBITORS**

Publication number: 20150099891

Abstract: Novel crystalline forms of (2R,3S,5R)-2-(2,5-Difluorophenyl)-5-[2-(methylsulfonyl)-2,6-dihydropyrrolo[3,4-c]pyrazol-5(4H)-yl]tetrahydro-2H-pyran-3-amine are potent inhibitors of dipeptidyl peptidase-IV and are useful for the treatment of non-insulin dependent (Type 2) diabetes mellitus. The invention also relates to pharmaceutical compositions containing these novel forms, processes to prepare these forms and their pharmaceutical compositions as well as uses thereof for the treatment of Type 2 diabetes.

Type: Application

Filed: October 6, 2014

Publication date: April 9, 2015

Inventors: Itzia Z. Arroyo, Davida Krueger, Ping Chen, Aaron J. Moment, Tesfaye Biftu, Faye Sheen, Yanfeng Zhang

- **PYRIDINE CGRP RECEPTOR ANTAGONISTS**

Publication number: 20150099771

Abstract: The present invention is directed to pyridine derivatives which are antagonists of CGRP receptors and useful in the treatment or prevention of diseases in which CGRP is involved, such as migraine. The invention is also directed to pharmaceutical compositions comprising these compounds and the use of these compounds and compositions in the prevention or treatment of such diseases in which CGRP is involved.

Type: Application

Filed: May 3, 2013

Publication date: April 9, 2015

Applicant: Merck Sharp & Dohme Corp.

Inventors: Ian M. Bell, Mark Fraley, Tesfaye Biftu, Cheng Zhu, Anilkumar Nair

- **HETEROCYCLIC CGRP RECEPTOR ANTAGONISTS**

Publication number: 20150087641

Abstract: The present invention is directed to heterocyclic compounds which are antagonists of CGRP receptors and useful in the treatment or prevention of diseases in which CGRP is involved, such as migraine. The invention is also directed to pharmaceutical compositions comprising these compounds and the use of these compounds and compositions in the prevention or treatment of such diseases in which CGRP is involved.

Type: Application

Filed: May 3, 2013

Publication date: March 26, 2015

Inventors: Ian M. Bell, Mark Fraley, Tesfaye Biftu, Cheng Zhu, Anilkumar Nair

- **Substituted seven-membered heterocyclic compounds as dipeptidyl peptidase-iv inhibitors for the treatment of diabetes**

Patent number: 8980929

Abstract: The present invention is directed to novel amino-substituted seven-membered heterocyclic compounds of structural formula (I) which are inhibitors of the dipeptidyl peptidase-IV enzyme and which are useful in the treatment or prevention of diseases in which the dipeptidyl peptidase-IV enzyme is involved, such as diabetes and particularly Type 2 diabetes. The invention is also directed to pharmaceutical compositions comprising these compounds and the use of these compounds and compositions in the prevention or treatment of such diseases in which the dipeptidyl peptidase-IV enzyme is involved.

Type: Grant

Filed: May 16, 2011

Date of Patent: March 17, 2015

Assignee: Merck Sharp & Dohme Corp.

Inventors: Jacqueline D. Hicks, Tesfaye Biftu, Ping Chen, Xiaoxia Qian, Robert R. Wilkening

- **Aminotetrahydropyrans as dipeptidyl peptidase-IV inhibitors for the treatment or prevention of diabetes**

Patent number: 8951965

Abstract: The present invention is directed to novel substituted aminotetrahydropyrans of structural formula I which are inhibitors of the dipeptidyl peptidase-IV enzyme and which are useful in the treatment or prevention of diseases in which the dipeptidyl peptidase-IV enzyme is involved, such as diabetes and particularly Type 2 diabetes. The invention is also directed to pharmaceutical compositions comprising these compounds and the use of these compounds and compositions in the prevention or treatment of such diseases in which the dipeptidyl peptidase-IV enzyme is involved.

Type: Grant

Filed: June 2, 2014

Date of Patent: February 10, 2015

Assignee: Merck Sharp & Dohme Corp.

Inventors: Tesfaye Biftu, Ann E. Weber

- **THROMBIN INHIBITORS**

Publication number: 20150038498

Abstract: Compounds of the invention are useful in inhibiting thrombin and associated thrombotic occlusions having the following structure: (I) or a pharmaceutically acceptable salt thereof, wherein Q is CH2, NR4, O, S, S(O) or S(O2), wherein R4 is H, C1-6 alkyl, aryl, or C3-8 cycloalkyl; R1 is a heterocycle or —(CR5R6)1-2NH2, wherein R5 and R6, each time in which they occur, are independently H, C1-6 alkyl, —CH2F, —CHF2, CF3 or —CH2OH; R2 is OH, NH2 or NHSO2CH3; and R3 is C1-6 alkyl.

Type: Application

Filed: March 22, 2013

Publication date: February 5, 2015

Inventors: Timothy Allen Blizzard, Tesfaye Biftu

- **PREPARATION AND USE OF BICYCLIC HIMBACINE DERIVATIVES AS PAR-1 RECEPTOR ANTAGONISTS**

Publication number: 20150025046

Abstract: The present invention relates to bicyclic himbacine derivatives of the formula or a pharmaceutically acceptable salt thereof, wherein: X is —O—, —N(R), —C(R8)(R9) or —C(O)—; and Y is —O—, —N(R), —C(R8)(R9) or —C(O)— and the remaining variables are described herein. The compounds of the invention are effective inhibitors of the PAR-1 receptor. The inventive compounds may be used for the treatment or prophylaxis of disease states such as ACS, secondary prevention of myocardial infarction or stroke, or PAD.

Type: Application

Filed: February 27, 2013

Publication date: January 22, 2015

Inventors: Mihir Mandal, Timothy A. Blizzard, Helen Chen, Harry Chobanian, Yan Guo, Barbara Pio, Zhicai Wu, Tesfaye Biftu, William J. Greenlee, Johnny Zhaoning Zhu

- **DIPEPTIDYL PEPTIDASE-IV INHIBITORS FOR THE TREATMENT OR PREVENTION OF DIABETES**

Publication number: 20150011590

Abstract: The present invention is directed to novel substituted dihydropyrrolopyrazoles of structural Formula I which are inhibitors of the dipeptidyl peptidase-IV enzyme and which are useful in the treatment or prevention of diseases in which the dipeptidyl peptidase-IV enzyme is involved, such as diabetes and particularly Type 2 diabetes. The invention is also directed to pharmaceutical compositions comprising these compounds and the use of these compounds and compositions in the prevention or treatment of such diseases in which the dipeptidyl peptidase-IV enzyme is involved.

Type: Application

Filed: February 12, 2013

Publication date: January 8, 2015

Applicant: Merck Sharp & Dohme Corporation

Inventors: Ann E. Weber, Tesfaye Biftu

- **Crystalline forms of a dipeptidyl peptidase-IV inhibitor**

Patent number: 8895603

Abstract: Novel crystalline forms of (2R,3S,5R)-2-(2,5-Difluorophenyl)-5-[2-(methylsulfonyl)-2,6-dihydropyrrolo[3,4-c]pyrazol-5(4H)-yl]tetrahydro-2H-pyran-3-amine are potent inhibitors of dipeptidyl peptidase-IV and are useful for the treatment of non-insulin dependent (Type 2) diabetes mellitus. The invention also relates to pharmaceutical compositions containing these novel forms, processes to prepare these forms and their pharmaceutical compositions as well as uses thereof for the treatment of Type 2 diabetes.

Type: Grant

Filed: June 25, 2012

Date of Patent: November 25, 2014

Assignees: Merck Sharp & Dohme Corp., Merck Sharp & Dohme Ltd.

Inventors: Itzia Arroyo, Davida Krueger, Ping Chen, Aaron Moment, Tesfaye Biftu, Faye Sheen, Yanfeng Zhang

- **Substituted aminotetrahydrothiopyrans and derivatives thereof as dipeptidyl peptidase-IV inhibitors for the treatment of diabetes**

Patent number: 8853212

Abstract: The present invention is directed to novel substituted aminotetrahydrothiopyrans and derivatives thereof of structural formula (I) which are inhibitors of the dipeptidyl peptidase-IV enzyme and which are useful in the treatment or prevention of diseases in which the dipeptidyl peptidase-IV enzyme is involved, such as diabetes and particularly Type 2 diabetes. The invention is also directed to pharmaceutical compositions comprising these compounds and the use of these compounds and compositions in the prevention or treatment of such diseases in which the dipeptidyl peptidase-IV enzyme is involved.

Type: Grant

Filed: February 17, 2011

Date of Patent: October 7, 2014

Assignee: Merck Sharp & Dohme Corp

Inventors: Robert R. Wilkening, James M. Apgar, Tesfaye Biftu, Danqing Feng, Xiaoxia Qian, Lan Wei

- **AMINOTETRAHYDROPYRANS AS DIPEPTIDYL PEPTIDASE-IV INHIBITORS FOR THE TREATMENT OR PREVENTION OF DIABETES**

Publication number: 20140287993

Abstract: The present invention is directed to novel substituted aminotetrahydropyrans of structural formula I which are inhibitors of the dipeptidyl peptidase-IV enzyme and which are useful in the treatment or prevention of diseases in which the dipeptidyl peptidase-IV enzyme is involved, such as diabetes and particularly Type 2 diabetes. The invention is also directed to pharmaceutical compositions comprising these compounds and the use of these compounds and compositions in the prevention or treatment of such diseases in which the dipeptidyl peptidase-IV enzyme is involved.

Type: Application

Filed: June 2, 2014

Publication date: September 25, 2014

Inventors: Tesfaye Biftu, Ann E. Weber

- <u>**Cyclic azabenzimidazole derivatives useful as anti-diabetic agents**</u>

Patent number: 8796258

Abstract: Novel compounds of structural formula (I) are activators of AMP-protein kinase and are useful in the treatment, prevention and suppression of diseases mediated by the AMPK-activated protein kinase. The compounds of the present invention are useful in the treatment of Type 2 diabetes, hyperglycemia, metabolic syndrome, obesity, hypercholesterolemia, and hypertension.

Type: Grant

Filed: February 23, 2012

Date of Patent: August 5, 2014

Assignee: Merck Sharp & Dohme Corp.

Inventors: Rajan Anand, James M. Apgar, Tesfaye Biftu, Ping Chen, Lin Chu, Vincent J. Colandrea, Guizhen Dong, James F. Dropinski, Danqing Feng, Jacqueline D. Hicks, Jinlong Jiang, Alexander J. Kim, Kenneth J. Leavitt, Bing Li, Xiaoxia Qian, Iyassu Sebhat, Lan Wei, Robert R. Wilkening, Zhicai Wu

- **Aminotetrahydropyrans as dipeptidyl peptidase-IV inhibitors for the treatment or prevention of diabetes**

Patent number: 8772328

Abstract: The present invention is directed to novel substituted aminotetrahydropyrans of structural formula I which are inhibitors of the dipeptidyl peptidase-IV enzyme and which are useful in the treatment or prevention of diseases in which the dipeptidyl peptidase-IV enzyme is involved, such as diabetes and particularly Type 2 diabetes. The invention is also directed to pharmaceutical compositions comprising these compounds and the use of these compounds and compositions in the prevention or treatment of such diseases in which the dipeptidyl peptidase-IV enzyme is involved.

Type: Grant

Filed: October 22, 2013

Date of Patent: July 8, 2014

Assignee: Merck Sharp & Dohme Corp.

Inventors: Tesfaye Biftu, Ann E. Weber

- **Substituted aminopiperidines as dipeptidyl peptidase-IV inhibitors for the treatment of diabetes**

Patent number: 8716482

Abstract: The present invention is directed to novel substituted aminopiperidines of structural formula I which are inhibitors of the dipeptidyl peptidase-IV enzyme and which are useful in the treatment or prevention of diseases in which the dipeptidyl peptidase-IV enzyme is involved, such as diabetes and particularly Type 2 diabetes. The invention is also directed to pharmaceutical compositions comprising these compounds and the use of these compounds and compositions in the prevention or treatment of such diseases in which the dipeptidyl peptidase-IV enzyme is involved.

Type: Grant

Filed: September 15, 2010

Date of Patent: May 6, 2014

Assignee: Merck Sharp & Dohme Corp.

Inventors: Jason M. Cox, Tesfaye Biftu, Hong Dong Chu, Danqing Feng, Ann E. Weber

- **NOVEL CRYSTALLINE FORMS OF A DIPEPTIDYL PEPTIDASE-IV INHIBITOR**

Publication number: 20140080884

Abstract: Novel crystalline forms of (2R,3S,5R)-2-(2,5-Difluorophenyl)-5-[2-(methylsulfonyl)-2,6-dihydropyrrolo[3,4-c]pyrazol-5(4H)-yl]tetrahydro-2H-pyran-3-amine are potent inhibitors of dipeptidyl peptidase-IV and are useful for the treatment of non-insulin dependent (Type 2) diabetes mellitus. The invention also relates to pharmaceutical compositions containing these novel forms, processes to prepare these forms and their pharmaceutical compositions as well as uses thereof for the treatment of Type 2 diabetes.

Type: Application

Filed: June 25, 2012

Publication date: March 20, 2014

Applicants: Merck Sharp & Dohme Ltd., Merck Sharp & Dohme Corp.

Inventors: Itzia Arroyo, Davida Krueger, Ping Chen, Aaron Moment, Tesfaye Biftu, Faye Sheen, Yanfeng Zhang

- <u>**AMINOTETRAHYDROPYRANS AS DIPEPTIDYL PEPTIDASE-IV INHIBITORS FOR THE TREATMENT OR PREVENTION OF DIABETES**</u>

Publication number: 20140051740

Abstract: The present invention is directed to novel substituted aminotetrahydropyrans of structural formula I which are inhibitors of the dipeptidyl peptidase-IV enzyme and which are useful in the treatment or prevention of diseases in which the dipeptidyl peptidase-IV enzyme is involved, such as diabetes and particularly Type 2 diabetes. The invention is also directed to pharmaceutical compositions comprising these compounds and the use of these compounds and compositions in the prevention or treatment of such diseases in which the dipeptidyl peptidase-IV enzyme is involved.

Type: Application

Filed: October 22, 2013

Publication date: February 20, 2014

Applicant: Merck Sharp & Dohme Corp.

Inventors: Tesfaye Biftu, Ann E. Weber

- **Heterocyclic compounds as dipeptidyl peptidase-IV inhibitors for the treatment or prevention of diabetes**

Patent number: 8653059

Abstract: The present invention is directed to substituted six-membered heterocyclic compounds of structural formula (I) which are inhibitors of the dipeptidyl peptidase-IV enzyme and which are useful in the treatment or prevention of diseases in which the dipeptidyl peptidase-IV enzyme is involved, such as obesity and diabetes, particularly Type 2 diabetes. The invention is also directed to pharmaceutical compositions comprising these compounds and the use of these compounds and compositions in the prevention or treatment of such diseases in which the dipeptidyl peptidase-IV enzyme is involved.

Type: Grant

Filed: August 18, 2008

Date of Patent: February 18, 2014

Assignee: Merck Sharp & Dohme Corp.

Inventors: Tesfaye Biftu, Danqing Feng, Ann E. Weber, Jason M. Cox, Xiaoxia Qian, Jinyou Xu

- **Aminotetrahydropyrans as dipeptidyl peptidase-IV inhibitors for the treatment or prevention of diabetes**

Patent number: 8592371

Abstract: The present invention is directed to novel substituted aminotetrahydropyrans of structural formula I which are inhibitors of the

dipeptidyl peptidase-IV enzyme and which are useful in the treatment or prevention of diseases in which the dipeptidyl peptidase-IV enzyme is involved, such as diabetes and particularly Type 2 diabetes. The invention is also directed to pharmaceutical compositions comprising these compounds and the use of these compounds and compositions in the prevention or treatment of such diseases in which the dipeptidyl peptidase-IV enzyme is involved.

Type: Grant

Filed: February 7, 2013

Date of Patent: November 26, 2013

Assignee: Merck Sharpe & Dohme Corp.

Inventors: Tesfaye Biftu, Ann E. Weber

- **SUBSTITUTED SEVEN-MEMBERED HETEROCYCLIC COMPOUNDS AS DIPEPTIDYL PEPTIDASE-IV INHIBITORS FOR THE TREATMENT OF DIABETES**

Publication number: 20130203786

Abstract: The present invention is directed to novel amino-substituted seven-membered heterocyclic compounds of structural formula (I) which are inhibitors of the dipeptidyl peptidase-IV enzyme and which are useful in the treatment or prevention of diseases in which the dipeptidyl peptidase-IV enzyme is involved, such as diabetes and particularly Type 2 diabetes. The invention is also directed to pharmaceutical compositions comprising these compounds and the use of these compounds and compositions in the prevention or treatment of such diseases in which the dipeptidyl peptidase-IV enzyme is involved.

Type: Application

Filed: May 16, 2011

Publication date: August 8, 2013

Inventors: Jacqueline D. Hicks, Tesfaye Biftu, Ping Chen, Xiaoxia Qian, Robert R. Wilkening

- **Aminotetrahydropyrans as dipeptidyl peptidase-IV inhibitors for the treatment or prevention of diabetes**

Patent number: 8455533

Abstract: The present invention is directed to novel substituted aminotetrahydropyrans of structural formula I which are inhibitors of the dipeptidyl peptidase-IV enzyme and which are useful in the treatment or prevention of diseases in which the dipeptidyl peptidase-IV enzyme is involved, such as diabetes and particularly Type 2 diabetes. The invention is also directed to pharmaceutical compositions comprising these compounds and the use of these compounds and compositions in the prevention or treatment of such diseases in which the dipeptidyl peptidase-IV enzyme is involved.

Type: Grant

Filed: August 23, 2010

Date of Patent: June 4, 2013

Assignee: Merck Sharp & Dohme Corp.

Inventors: Tesfaye Biftu, Ping Chen, Danqing Feng, Xiaoxia Qian

- **NOVEL CYCLIC AZABENZIMIDAZOLE DERIVATIVES USEFUL AS ANTI-DIABETIC AGENTS**

Publication number: 20130123237

Abstract: Novel compounds of structural formula (I) are activators of AMP-protein kinase and are useful in the treatment, prevention and suppression of diseases mediated by the AMPK-activated protein kinase. The compounds of the present invention are useful in the treatment of Type 2 diabetes, hyperglycemia, metabolic syndrome, obesity, hypercholesterolemia, and hypertension.

Type: Application

Filed: February 23, 2012

Publication date: May 16, 2013

Applicant: Merck Sharp & Dohme Corp.

Inventors: Rajan Anand, James M. Apgar, Tesfaye Biftu, Ping Chen, Lin Chu, Vincent J. Colandrea, Guizhen Dong, James F. Dropinski, Danqing Feng, Jacqueline D. Hicks, Jinlong Jiang, Alexander J. Kim, Kenneth J. Leavitt, Bing Li, Xiaoxia Qian, Iyassu Sebhat, Lan Wei, Robert R. Wilkening, Zhicai Wu

- **Aminotetrahydropyrans as dipeptidyl peptidase-IV inhibitors for the treatment or prevention of diabetes**

Patent number: 8415297

Abstract: The present invention is directed to novel substituted aminotetrahydropyrans of structural formula I which are inhibitors of the dipeptidyl peptidase-IV enzyme and which are useful in the treatment or

prevention of diseases in which the dipeptidyl peptidase-IV enzyme is involved, such as diabetes and particularly Type 2 diabetes. The invention is also directed to pharmaceutical compositions comprising these compounds and the use of these compounds and compositions in the prevention or treatment of such diseases in which the dipeptidyl peptidase-IV enzyme is involved.

Type: Grant

Filed: February 17, 2012

Date of Patent: April 9, 2013

Assignee: Merck Sharp & Dohme Corp.

Inventors: Tesfaye Biftu, Ann E. Weber

- **SUBSTITUTED AMINOTETRAHYDROTHIOPYRANS AND DERIVATIVES THEREOF AS DIPEPTIDYL PEPTIDASE-IV INHIBITORS FOR THE TREATMENT OF DIABETES**

Publication number: 20120277240

Abstract: The present invention is directed to novel substituted aminotetrahydrothiopyrans and derivatives thereof of structural formula (I) which are inhibitors of the dipeptidyl peptidase-IV enzyme and which are useful in the treatment or prevention of diseases in which the dipeptidyl peptidase-IV enzyme is involved, such as diabetes and particularly Type 2 diabetes. The invention is also directed to pharmaceutical compositions comprising these compounds and the use of these compounds and compositions in the prevention or treatment of such diseases in which the dipeptidyl peptidase-IV enzyme is involved.

Type: Application

Filed: February 17, 2011

Publication date: November 1, 2012

Inventors: Robert R. Wilkening, James M. Apgar, Tesfaye Biftu, Danqing Feng, Xiaoxia Qian, Lan Wei

- **AMINOTETRAHYDROPYRANS AS DIPEPTIDYL PEPTIDASE-IV INHIBITORS FOR THE TREATMENT OR PREVENTION OF DIABETES**

Publication number: 20120149734

Abstract: The present invention is directed to novel substituted aminotetrahydropyrans of structural formula I which are inhibitors of the dipeptidyl peptidase-IV enzyme and which are useful in the treatment or prevention of diseases in which the dipeptidyl peptidase-IV enzyme is involved, such as diabetes and particularly Type 2 diabetes. The invention is also directed to pharmaceutical compositions comprising these compounds and the use of these compounds and compositions in the prevention or treatment of such diseases in which the dipeptidyl peptidase-IV enzyme is involved.

Type: Application

Filed: August 23, 2010

Publication date: June 14, 2012

Inventors: Tesfaye Biftu, Ping Chen, Danqing Feng, Xiaoxia Qian

- **AMINOTETRAHYDROPYRANS AS DIPEPTIDYL PEPTIDASE-IV INHIBITORS FOR THE TREATMENT OR PREVENTION OF DIABETES**

Publication number: 20120149637

Abstract: The present invention is directed to novel substituted aminotetrahydropyrans of structural formula I which are inhibitors of the dipeptidyl peptidase-IV enzyme and which are useful in the treatment or prevention of diseases in which the dipeptidyl peptidase-IV enzyme is involved, such as diabetes and particularly Type 2 diabetes. The invention is also directed to pharmaceutical compositions comprising these compounds and the use of these compounds and compositions in the prevention or treatment of such diseases in which the dipeptidyl peptidase-IV enzyme is involved.

Type: Application

Filed: February 17, 2012

Publication date: June 14, 2012

Inventors: Tesfaye Biftu, Ping Chen, Jason M. Cox, Ann E. Weber

- **SUBSTITUTED AMINOPIPERIDINES AS DIPEPTIDYL PEPTIDASE-IV INHIBITORS FOR THE TREATMENT OF DIABETES**

Publication number: 20120149683

Abstract: The present invention is directed to novel substituted aminopiperidines of structural formula I which are inhibitors of the dipeptidyl peptidase-IV enzyme and which are useful in the treatment or prevention of diseases in which the dipeptidyl peptidase-IV enzyme is involved, such as diabetes and particularly Type 2 diabetes. The invention is also directed to pharmaceutical compositions comprising these compounds and the use of these compounds and compositions in the prevention or treatment of such diseases in which the dipeptidyl peptidase-IV enzyme is involved.

Type: Application

Filed: September 15, 2010

Publication date: June 14, 2012

Inventors: Jason M. Cox, Tesfaye Biftu, Hong Dong Chu, Danqing Feng, Ann E. Weber

- **Aminotetrahydropyrans as dipeptidyl peptidase-IV inhibitors for the treatment or prevention of diabetes**

Patent number: 8143289

Abstract: The present invention is directed to novel substituted aminotetrahydropyrans of structural formula I which are inhibitors of the dipeptidyl peptidase-IV enzyme and which are useful in the treatment or prevention of diseases in which the dipeptidyl peptidase-IV enzyme is involved, such as diabetes and particularly Type 2 diabetes. The invention is also directed to pharmaceutical compositions comprising these compounds and the use of these compounds and compositions in the prevention or treatment of such diseases in which the dipeptidyl peptidase-IV enzyme is involved.

Type: Grant

Filed: November 12, 2009

Date of Patent: March 27, 2012

Assignee: Merck Sharp & Dohme Corp.

Inventors: Tesfaye Biftu, Ping Chen, Jason M. Cox, Ann E. Weber

- **HETEROCYCLIC COMPOUNDS AS DIPEPTIDYL PEPTIDASE-IV INHIBITORS FOR THE TREATMENT OR PREVENTION OF DIABETES**

Publication number: 20110224195

Abstract: The present invention is directed to substituted six-membered heterocyclic compounds of structural formula (I) which are inhibitors of the dipeptidyl peptidase-IV enzyme and which are useful in the treatment or prevention of diseases in which the dipeptidyl peptidase-IV enzyme is involved, such as obesity and diabetes, particularly Type 2 diabetes. The invention is also directed to pharmaceutical compositions comprising these compounds and the use of these compounds and compositions in the prevention or treatment of such diseases in which the dipeptidyl peptidase-IV enzyme is involved.

Type: Application

Filed: August 18, 2008

Publication date: September 15, 2011

Inventors: Tesfaye Biftu, Danqing Feng, Ann E. Weber, Jason M. Cox, Xiaoxia Qian, Jinyou Xu

- **Substituted 5,6,7,8-tetrahydropyrido[4,3-D]pyrimidines as dipeptidyl peptidase-IV inhibitors for the treatment or prevention of diabetes**

Patent number: 7928112

Abstract: The present invention is directed to novel substituted aminotetrahydropyrans of structural formula I which are inhibitors of the dipeptidyl peptidase-IV enzyme and which are useful in the treatment or prevention of diseases in which the dipeptidyl peptidase-IV enzyme is involved, such as diabetes and particularly Type 2 diabetes. The invention is also directed to pharmaceutical compositions comprising these compounds and the use of these compounds and compositions in the prevention or treatment of such diseases in which the dipeptidyl peptidase-IV enzyme is involved.

Type: Grant

Filed: August 27, 2010

Date of Patent: April 19, 2011

Assignee: Merck Sharp & Dohme Corp.

Inventors: Tesfaye Biftu, Ping Chen, Danqing Feng, Ann E. Weber

- **Aminotetrahydropyrans as dipeptidyl peptidase-IV inhibitors for the treatment or prevention of diabetes**

Patent number: 7910596

Abstract: The present invention is directed to novel substituted aminotetrahydropyrans of structural formula I which are inhibitors of the dipeptidyl peptidase-IV enzyme and which are useful in the treatment or

prevention of diseases in which the dipeptidyl peptidase-IV enzyme is involved, such as diabetes and particularly Type 2 diabetes. The invention is also directed to pharmaceutical compositions comprising these compounds and the use of these compounds and compositions in the prevention or treatment of such diseases in which the dipeptidyl peptidase-IV enzyme is involved.

Type: Grant

Filed: February 9, 2007

Date of Patent: March 22, 2011

Assignee: Merck Sharp & Dohme Corp.

Inventors: Tesfaye Biftu, Charles G Caldwell, Ann E. Weber, Ping P Chen, Xiaoxia Qian, Danqing Feng, Jason M. Cox

- **<u>Aminocyclohexanes as dipeptidyl peptidase-IV inhibitors for the treatment of diabetes</u>**

Patent number: 7906649

Abstract: The present invention is directed to novel substituted aminocyclohexanes which are inhibitors of the dipeptidyl peptidase-IV enzyme ("DPP-IV inhibitors") and which are useful in the treatment or prevention of diseases in which the dipeptidyl peptidase-IV enzyme is involved, such as diabetes and particularly Type 2 diabetes. The invention is also directed to pharmaceutical compositions comprising these compounds and the use of these compounds and compositions in the prevention or treatment of such diseases in which the dipeptidyl peptidase-IV enzyme is involved.

Type: Grant

Filed: May 19, 2006

Date of Patent: March 15, 2011

Assignee: Merck Sharp & Dohme Corp.

Inventors: Tesfaye Biftu, Danqing Feng, Xiaoxia Qian, Ann E. Weber, Jason Cox

- **AMINOTETRAHYDROPYRANS AS DIPEPTIDYL PEPTIDASE-IV INHIBITORS FOR THE TREATMENT OR PREVENTION OF DIABETES**

Publication number: 20100324054

Abstract: The present invention is directed to novel substituted aminotetrahydropyrans of structural formula I which are inhibitors of the dipeptidyl peptidase-IV enzyme and which are useful in the treatment or prevention of diseases in which the dipeptidyl peptidase-IV enzyme is involved, such as diabetes and particularly Type 2 diabetes. The invention is also directed to pharmaceutical compositions comprising these compounds and the use of these compounds and compositions in the prevention or treatment of such diseases in which the dipeptidyl peptidase-IV enzyme is involved.

Type: Application

Filed: August 27, 2010

Publication date: December 23, 2010

Inventors: Tesfaye Biftu, Ping Chen, Danqing Feng, Ann E. Weber

- **Substitued [1,2,4]triazolo[1,5-a]pyrazines as dipeptidyl peptidase-IV inhibitors for the treatment or prevention of diabetes**

Patent number: 7812027

Abstract: The present invention is directed to novel substituted aminotetrahydropyrans of structural formula I which are inhibitors of the dipeptidyl peptidase-IV enzyme and which are useful in the treatment or prevention of diseases in which the dipeptidyl peptidase-IV enzyme is involved, such as diabetes and particularly Type 2 diabetes. The invention is also directed to pharmaceutical compositions comprising these compounds and the use of these compounds and compositions in the prevention or treatment of such diseases in which the dipeptidyl peptidase-IV enzyme is involved.

Type: Grant

Filed: May 11, 2007

Date of Patent: October 12, 2010

Assignee: Merck Sharp & Dohme Corp.

Inventors: Tesfaye Biftu, Ping Chen, Danqing Feng, Ann E. Weber

- **Aminotetrahydropyrans as Dipeptidyl Peptidase-IV Inhibitors for the Treatment or Prevention of Diabetes**

Publication number: 20100234403

Abstract: The present invention is directed to novel substituted aminotetrahydropyrans of structural formula I which are inhibitors of the

dipeptidyl peptidase-IV enzyme and which are useful in the treatment or prevention of diseases in which the dipeptidyl peptidase-IV enzyme is involved, such as diabetes and particularly Type 2 diabetes. The invention is also directed to pharmaceutical compositions comprising these compounds and the use of these compounds and compositions in the prevention or treatment of such diseases in which the dipeptidyl peptidase-IV enzyme is involved.

Type: Application

Filed: February 9, 2007

Publication date: September 16, 2010

Inventors: Tesfaye Biftu, Charles G. Caldwell, Ann E. Weber, Ping Chen, Xiaoxia Qian, Danqing Feng, Jason M. Cox

- **Aminocyclohexanes as dipeptidyl peptidase-IV inhibitors for the treatment or prevention of diabetes**

Patent number: 7750034

Abstract: The present invention is directed to novel substituted aminocyclohexanes of structural formula (I) which are inhibitors of the dipeptidyl peptidase-IV enzyme and which are useful in the treatment or prevention of diseases in which the dipeptidyl peptidase-IV enzyme is involved, such as diabetes and particularly Type 2 diabetes. The invention is also directed to pharmaceutical compositions comprising these compounds and the use of these compounds and compositions in the prevention or treatment of such diseases in which the dipeptidyl peptidase-IV enzyme is involved.

Type: Grant

Filed: January 19, 2007

Date of Patent: July 6, 2010

Assignee: Merck Sharp & Dohme Corp.

Inventors: Tesfaye Biftu, Jason Cox, Danqing Feng, Anthony Mastracchio, Xiaoxia Qian, Ann E. Weber

- **AMINOTETRAHYDROPYRANS AS DIPEPTIDYL PEPTIDASE-IV INHIBITORS FOR THE TREATMENT OR PREVENTION OF DIABETES**

Publication number: 20100120863

Abstract: The present invention is directed to novel substituted aminotetrahydropyrans of structural formula I which are inhibitors of the dipeptidyl peptidase-IV enzyme and which are useful in the treatment or prevention of diseases in which the dipeptidyl peptidase-IV enzyme is involved, such as diabetes and particularly Type 2 diabetes. The invention is also directed to pharmaceutical compositions comprising these compounds and the use of these compounds and compositions in the prevention or treatment of such diseases in which the dipeptidyl peptidase-IV enzyme is involved.

Type: Application

Filed: November 12, 2009

Publication date: May 13, 2010

Inventors: Tesfaye Biftu, Ping Chen, Jason M. Cox, Ann E. Weber

- **Aminotetrahydropyrans as dipeptidyl peptidase-IV inhibitors for the treatment or prevention of diabetes**

Patent number: 7678905

Abstract: The present invention is directed to novel substituted aminotetrahydropyrans of structural formula I which are inhibitors of the dipeptidyl peptidase-IV enzyme and which are useful in the treatment or prevention of diseases in which the dipeptidyl peptidase-IV enzyme is involved, such as diabetes and particularly Type 2 diabetes. The invention is also directed to pharmaceutical compositions comprising these compounds and the use of these compounds and compositions in the prevention or treatment of such diseases in which the dipeptidyl peptidase-IV enzyme is involved.

Type: Grant

Filed: March 27, 2007

Date of Patent: March 16, 2010

Assignee: Merck Sharp & Dohme Corp.

Inventors: Tesfaye Biftu, Ann E. Weber

- **Aminocyclohexanes as Dipeptidyl Peptidase-IV Inhibitors for the Treatment or Prevention of Diabetes**

Publication number: 20090270467

Abstract: The present invention is directed to novel substituted aminocyclohexanes of structural formula (I) which are inhibitors of the dipeptidyl peptidase-IV enzyme and which are useful in the treatment or prevention of diseases in which the dipeptidyl peptidase-IV enzyme is involved, such as diabetes and particularly Type 2 diabetes. The invention is also directed to pharmaceutical compositions comprising these compounds and the use of these compounds and compositions in the prevention or treatment of such diseases in which the dipeptidyl peptidase-IV enzyme is involved.

Type: Application

Filed: January 19, 2007

Publication date: October 29, 2009

Applicant: MERCK & CO., INC.

Inventors: Tesfaye Biftu, Jason Cox, Danqing Feng, Anthony Mastracchio, Xiaoxia Qian, Ann E. Weber

- **Aminotetrahydropyrans as Dipeptidyl Peptidase-IV Inhibitors for the Treatment or Prevention of Diabetes**

Publication number: 20090209544

Abstract: The present invention is directed to novel substituted aminotetrahydropyrans of structural formula I which are inhibitors of the dipeptidyl peptidase-IV enzyme and which are useful in the treatment or prevention of diseases in which the dipeptidyl peptidase-IV enzyme is involved, such as diabetes and particularly Type 2 diabetes. The invention is also directed to pharmaceutical compositions comprising these compounds and the use of these compounds and compositions in the prevention or treatment of such diseases in which the dipeptidyl peptidase-IV enzyme is involved.

Type: Application

Filed: May 11, 2007

Publication date: August 20, 2009

Inventors: Tesfaye Biftu, Ping Chen, Danqing Feng, Ann E. Weber

- <u>3-Amino-4-phenylbutanoic acid derivatives as dipeptidyl peptidase inhibitors for the treatment or prevention of diabetes</u>

Patent number: 7560455

Abstract: The pre-sent invention is directed to 3-amino-4-phenylbutanoic acid derivatives which are inhibitors of the dipeptidyl peptidase-IV enzyme ("DP-IV inhibitors") and which are useful in the treatment or prevention of diseases in which the dipeptidyl peptidase-IV enzyme is involved, such as diabetes and particularly type 2 diabetes. The invention is also directed to pharmaceutical compositions comprising these compounds and the use of these compounds and compositions in the prevention or treatment of such diseases in which the dipeptidyl peptidase-IV enzyme is involved.

Type: Grant

Filed: May 10, 2004

Date of Patent: July 14, 2009

Assignee: Merck & Co., Inc.

Inventors: Tesfaye Biftu, Danqing Dennis Feng, Gui Bai Liang, Xiaoxia Qian

- **Aminocyclohexanes as Dipeptidyl Peptidase-IV for the Treatment or Prevention of Diabetes**

Publication number: 20090105284

Abstract: The present invention is directed to novel substituted aminocyclohexanes which are inhibitors of the dipeptidyl peptidase-IV enzyme ("DPP-IV inhibitors") and which are useful in the treatment or prevention of diseases in which the dipeptidyl peptidase-IV enzyme is involved, such as diabetes and particularly Type 2 diabetes. The invention is also directed to pharmaceutical compositions comprising these compounds and the use of these compounds and compositions in the prevention or treatment of such diseases in which the dipeptidyl peptidase-IV enzyme is involved.

Type: Application

Filed: May 19, 2006

Publication date: April 23, 2009

Applicant: MERCK & CO., INC.

Inventors: Tesfaye Biftu, Danqing Feng, Xiaoxia Qian, Ann E. Weber, Jason Cox

- **Antiprotozoal imidazopyridine compounds**

Patent number: 7504501

Abstract: Compounds described by the Formula (I): (I) or pharmaceutically acceptable salts, or N-oxides thereof. The compounds are useful for the treatment and prevention of protozoal diseases in mammals and birds. A method for controlling coccidiosis in poultry comprises administering an effective amount of the compound alone, or in combination with one or more anticoccidial agent(s). A composition for controlling coccidiosis in poultry comprises the compound alone, or in combination with one or more anticoccidial agent(s). Methods for the treatment and prevention of mammalian protozoal diseases, such as, for example, toxoplasmosis, malaria, African trypanosomiasis, Chagas disease, and opportunistic infections comprise administering the compound alone, or in combination with one or more antiprotozoal agent(s).

Type: Grant

Filed: March 2, 2004

Date of Patent: March 17, 2009

Assignee: Merial Limited

Inventors: Matthew J. Wyvratt, Tesfaye Biftu, Michael H. Fisher, Dennis M. Schmatz

- **Aminocyclohexanes as dipeptidyl peptidase-IV inhibitors for the treatment or prevention of diabetes**

Patent number: 7482336

Abstract: The present invention is directed to novel substituted aminocyclohexanes which are inhibitors of the dipeptidyl peptidase-IV enzyme ("DPP-IV inhibitors") and which are useful in the treatment or prevention of diseases in which the dipeptidyl peptidase-IV enzyme is involved, such as diabetes and particularly Type 2 diabetes. The invention is also directed to pharmaceutical compositions comprising these compounds and the use of these compounds and compositions in the prevention or treatment of such diseases in which the dipeptidyl peptidase-IV enzyme is involved.

Type: Grant

Filed: June 17, 2005

Date of Patent: January 27, 2009

Assignee: Merck & Co., Inc.

Inventors: Tesfaye Biftu, Danqing Feng, Ying-Duo Gao, Suresh Singh, Ann E. Weber

- **Antiprotozoal imidazopyridine compounds**

Patent number: 7429590

Abstract: Compounds described by the Formula (I) or (II): or pharmaceutically acceptable salts, or N-oxides thereof. The compounds are useful for the treatment and prevention of protozoal diseases in mammals and birds. A method for controlling coccidiosis in poultry comprises administering an effective amount of the compound alone, or in combination with one or more anticoccidieal agent(s). A composition for controlling coccidiosis in poultry comprises the compound alone, or in combination with one or more anticoccidial agent(s). Methods for the treatment and prevention of mammalian protozoal diseases, such as, for example, toxoplasmosis, malaria. African typanosomiasis, Chagas disease, and opportunistic infections comprise administering the compound alone, or in combination with one or more antiprotozoal agent(s).

Type: Grant

Filed: December 6, 2004

Date of Patent: September 30, 2008

Assignee: Merck & Co. Inc.

Inventors: Tesfaye Biftu, Matthew J. Wyvratt, Louis L. Zuegner, III, legal representative, Michael H. Fisher

- **Aminocyclohexanes as Dipeptidyl Peptidase-Iv Inhibitors for the Treatment or Prevention of Diabetes**

Publication number: 20070254865

Abstract: The present invention is directed to novel substituted aminocyclohexanes which are inhibitors of the dipeptidyl peptidase-IV enzyme ("DPP-IV inhibitors") and which are useful in the treatment or prevention of diseases in which the dipeptidyl peptidase-IV enzyme is involved, such as diabetes and particularly Type 2 diabetes. The invention is also directed to pharmaceutical compositions comprising these compounds and the use of these compounds and compositions in the prevention or treatment of such diseases in which the dipeptidyl peptidase-IV enzyme is involved.

Type: Application

Filed: June 17, 2005

Publication date: November 1, 2007

Inventors: Tesfaye Biftu, Danqing Feng, Ying-Duo Gao, Suresh Singh, Ann Weber

- **Aminotetrahydropyrans as dipeptidyl peptidase-IV inhibitors for the treatment or prevention of diabetes**

Publication number: 20070232676

Abstract: The present invention is directed to novel substituted aminotetrahydropyrans of structural formula I which are inhibitors of the dipeptidyl peptidase-IV enzyme and which are useful in the treatment or prevention of diseases in which the dipeptidyl peptidase-IV enzyme is involved, such as diabetes and particularly Type 2 diabetes. The invention is also directed to pharmaceutical compositions comprising these compounds and the use of these compounds and compositions in the prevention or treatment of such diseases in which the dipeptidyl peptidase-IV enzyme is involved.

Type: Application

Filed: March 27, 2007

Publication date: October 4, 2007

Inventors: Tesfaye Biftu, Ann E. Weber

- **Hexahydrodiazepinones as dipeptidyl peptidase-IV inhibitors for the treatment or prevention of diabetes**

Patent number: 7259160

Abstract: The present invention is directed to hexahydrodiazepinone compounds which are inhibitors of the dipeptidyl peptidase-IV enzyme

("DPP-IV inhibitors") and which are useful in the treatment or prevention of diseases in which the dipeptidyl peptidase-IV enzyme is involved, such as diabetes and particularly type 2 diabetes. The invention is also directed to pharmaceutical compositions comprising these compounds and the use of these compounds and compositions in the prevention or treatment of such diseases in which the dipeptidyl peptidase-IV enzyme is involved.

Type: Grant

Filed: July 27, 2004

Date of Patent: August 21, 2007

Assignee: Merck & Co., Inc.

Inventors: Gui-Bai Liang, Tesfaye Biftu, Danqing Dennis Feng, Ann E. Weber

- **(Pyrimidinyl) (phenyl) substituted fused heteroaryl p38 inhibiting and PKG kinase inhibiting compounds**

Patent number: 7196095

Abstract: Compounds of formula (I) and pharmaceutically acceptable salts thereof are useful in the treatment of cytokine mediated diseases such as arthritis and in the treatment and/or prevention of protozoal diseases such as coccidiosis

Type: Grant

Filed: June 21, 2002

Date of Patent: March 27, 2007

Assignee: Merck & Co., Inc.

Inventors: Tesfaye Biftu, Richard Beresis, Richard Berger, Steven L. Colletti, James B. Doherty, Dennis D. Feng, Gui-Bai Liang, Dennis M. Schmatz, Xiaoxia Qian, David A. Claremon, Nigel J. Liverton, Charles J. McIntyre, Ernest W. Kovacs

- **<u>Antiprotozoal imidazopyridine compounds</u>**

Publication number: 20060293303

Abstract: Compounds described by the Formula (I) or (II): or pharmaceutically acceptable salts, or N-oxides thereof. The compounds are useful for the treatment and prevention of protozoal diseases in mammals and birds. A method for controlling coccidiosis in poultry comprises administering an effective amount of the compound alone, or in combination with one or more anticoccidieal agent(s). A composition for controlling coccidiosis in poultry comprises the compound alone, or in combination with one or more anticoccidial agent(s). Methods for the treatment and prevention of mammalian protozoal diseases, such as, for example, toxoplasmosis, malaria. African typanosomiasis, Chagas disease, and opportunistic infections comprise administering the compound alone, or in combination with one or more antiprotozoal agent(s).

Type: Application

Filed: December 6, 2004

Publication date: December 28, 2006

Inventors: Tesfaye Biftu, Matthew Wyvratt, Michael Fisher

- **3-Amino-4-phenylbutanoic acid derivatives as dipeptidyl peptidase inhibitors for the treatment or prevention of diabetes**

Publication number: 20060258646

Abstract: The pre-sent invention is directed to 3-amino-4-phenylbutanoic acid derivatives which are inhibitors of the dipeptidyl peptidase-IV enzyme ("DP-IV inhibitors") and which are useful in the treatment or prevention of diseases in which the dipeptidyl peptidase-IV enzyme is involved, such as diabetes and particularly type 2 diabetes. The invention is also directed to pharmaceutical compositions comprising these compounds and the use of these compounds and compositions in the prevention or treatment of such diseases in which the dipeptidyl peptidase-IV enzyme is involved.

Type: Application

Filed: May 10, 2004

Publication date: November 16, 2006

Inventors: Tesfaye Biftu, Danqing Feng, Gui Liang, Xiaoxia Qian

- **Hexahydrodiazepinones as dipeptidyl peptidase-iv inhibitors for the treatment or prevention of diabetes**

Publication number: 20060211682

Abstract: The present invention is directed to hexahydrodiazepinone compounds which are inhibitors of the dipeptidyl peptidase-IV enzyme ("DPP-IV inhibitors") and which are useful in the treatment or

prevention of diseases in which the dipeptidyl peptidase-IV enzyme is involved, such as diabetes and particularly type 2 diabetes. The invention is also directed to pharmaceutical compositions comprising these compounds and the use of these compounds and compositions in the prevention or treatment of such diseases in which the dipeptidyl peptidase-IV enzyme is involved.

Type: Application

Filed: July 27, 2004

Publication date: September 21, 2006

Inventors: Gui-Bai Liang, Tesfaye Biftu, Danqing Feng, Ann Weber

- **Beta-amino heterocyclic dipeptidyl peptidase inhibitors for the treatment or prevention of diabetes**

Patent number: 7101871

Abstract: The present invention is directed to compounds which are inhibitors of the dipeptidyl peptidase-IV enzyme ("DP-IV inhibitors") and which are useful in the treatment or prevention of diseases in which the dipeptidyl peptidase-IV enzyme is involved, such as diabetes and particularly type 2 diabetes. The invention is also directed to pharmaceutical compositions comprising these compounds and the use of these compounds and compositions in the prevention or treatment of such diseases in which the dipeptidyl peptidase-IV enzyme is involved.

Type: Grant

Filed: October 14, 2003

Date of Patent: September 5, 2006

Assignee: Merck & Co., Inc.

Inventors: Tesfaye Biftu, Gui-Bai Liang, Xiaoxia Qian, Ann E. Weber, Danqing Dennis Feng

- **Antiprotozoal imidazopyridine compounds**

Publication number: 20060178358

Abstract: Compounds described by the Formula (I): (I) or pharmaceutically acceptable salts, or N-oxides thereof. The compounds are useful for the treatment and prevention of protozoal diseases in mammals and birds. A method for controlling coccidiosis in poultry comprises administering an effective amount of the compound alone, or in combination with one or more anticoccidial agent(s). A composition for controlling coccidiosis in poultry comprises the compound alone, or in combination with one or more anticoccidial agent(s). Methods for the treatment and prevention of mammalian protozoal diseases, such as, for example, toxoplasmosis, malaria, African trypanosomiasis, Chagas disease, and opportunistic infections comprise administering the compound alone, or in combination with one or more antiprotozoal agent(s).

Type: Application

Filed: March 2, 2004

Publication date: August 10, 2006

Inventors: Matthew Wyvratt, Tesfaye Biftu, Michael Fisher, Dennis Schmatz

- **Beta-amino heterocyclic dipeptidyl peptidase inhibitors for the treatment or prevention of diabetes**

Publication number: 20040254167

Abstract: The present invention is directed to compounds which are inhibitors of the dipeptidyl peptidase-IV enzyme ("DP-IV inhibitors") and which are useful in the treatment or prevention of diseases in which the dipeptidyl peptidase-IV enzyme is involved, such as diabetes and particularly type 2 diabetes. The invention is also directed to pharmaceutical compositions comprising these compound and the use of these compounds and compositions in the prevention or treatment of such diseases in which the dipeptidyl peptidase-IV enzyme is involved.

Type: Application

Filed: July 9, 2004

Publication date: December 16, 2004

Inventors: Tesfaye Biftu, Gui-Bai Liang, Xiaoxia Qian, Ann E. Weber, Danqing Dennis Feng

- **(Pyrimidinyl) (phenyl) substituted fused heteroaryl p38 inhibiting and pkg kinase inhibiting compounds**

Publication number: 20040176396

Abstract: Compounds of formula (I) and pharmaceutically acceptable salts thereof are useful in the treatment of cytokine mediated diseases such as arthritis and in the treatment and/or prevention of protozoal diseases such as coccidiosis.

Type: Application

Filed: November 12, 2003

Publication date: September 9, 2004

Inventors: Tesfaye Biftu, Richard Beresis, Richard Berger, Steven L Coletti, James B Doherty, Dennis D Feng, Gui-Bai Liang, Dennis M Schmatz, Xiaoxia Qian, David A Claremon, Nigel J Liverton, Charles J McIntyre, Ernest W Kovacs

- **Aliphatic amine substituted piperidyl diaryl pyrrole derivatives as antiprotozoal agents**

Patent number: 6432980

Abstract: Trisubstituted pyrroles are antiprotozoal agents useful in the treatment and prevention of protozoal diseases in human and animals, including the control of coccidiosis in poultry.

Type: Grant

Filed: November 10, 2000

Date of Patent: August 13, 2002

Assignee: Merck & Co., Inc.

Inventors: Tesfaye Biftu, Danqing D. Feng, Gui-Bai Liang, Mitree M. Ponpipom, Xiaoxia Qian, Narindar Girotra, Michael H. Fischer, Matthew J. Wyvratt

- **Compounds and methods for the treatment of cardiovascular, inflammatory and immune disorders**

Patent number: 6420392

Abstract: 2,5-Diaryl tetrahydrofurans, 2,5-diaryl tetrahydrothiophenes, 1,3-diaryl cyclopentanes are disclosed that reduce the chemotaxis and respiratory burst leading to the formation of damaging oxygen radicals of polymorphonuclear leukocytes during an inflammatory or immune response. The compounds exhibit this biological activity by acting as PAF receptor antagonists, by inhibiting the enzyme 5-lipoxygenase, or by exhibiting dual activity, i.e., by acting as both a PAF receptor antagonist and inhibitor of 5-lipoxygenase. Also disclosed is a method to treat disorders mediated by PAF and/or leukotrienes that includes administering an effective amount of one or more of the above-identified compounds or a pharmaceutically acceptable salt thereof, optionally in a pharmaceutically acceptable carrier, to a patient in need of such therapy.

Type: Grant

Filed: October 9, 1996

Date of Patent: July 16, 2002

Assignee: Millennium Pharmaceuticals, Inc.

Inventors: Tesfaye Biftu, Xiong Cai, Sajjat Hussoin, Gurmit Grewal, T Y Shen

- **Diaryl piperidyl pyrrole derivatives as antiprotozoal agents**

Patent number: 6291480

Abstract: Trisubstituted pyrroles are antiprotozoal agents useful in the treatment and prevention of protozoal diseases in human and animals, including the control of coccidiosis in poultry.

Type: Grant

Filed: November 10, 2000

Date of Patent: September 18, 2001

Assignee: Merck & Co., Inc.

Inventors: Tesfaye Biftu, Danqing Dennis Feng, Gui-Bai Liang, Mitree M. Ponpipom, Xiaoxia Qian, Michael H. Fisher, Matthew J. Wyvratt

- **Compounds and methods for the treatment of cardiovascular, inflammatory and immune disorders**

Patent number: 6201016

Abstract: Enantiomerically enriched disubstituted tetrahydrofurans, tetrahydrothiophenes, pyrrolidines and cyclopentanes are disclosed that reduce the chemotaxis and respiratory burst leading to the formation of damaging oxygen radicals of polymorphonuclear leukocytes during an inflammatory or immune response. The compounds exhibit this biological activity by acting as PAF receptor antagonists, by inhibiting the enzyme 5-lipoxygenase, or by exhibiting dual activity, i. e., by acting as both a PAF receptor antagonist and inhibitor of 5-lipoxygenase. It has been determined that 5-lipoxygenase activity, oral availability, and stability in vivo (for example, glucuronidation rate) can vary significantly among the optical isomers of the disclosed compounds.

Type: Grant

Filed: February 17, 1995

Date of Patent: March 13, 2001

Assignee: CytoMed Incorporated

Inventors: Xiong Cai, Gurmit Grewal, Sajjat Hussoin, Aberra Fura, Ralph Scannell, Tesfaye Biftu

- **Epibatidine and derivatives thereof as nicotine cholinergic receptor agonists**

Patent number: 6177451

Abstract: The present invention provides methods of treatment utilizing pharmaceutical compositions comprising an effective nicotine agonist amount of epibatidine (1) or a synthetic 7-azabicyclo[2.2.1]-heptane or heptene derivative thereof, and a pharmaceutically acceptable earner, excipient or diluent.

Type: Grant

Filed: June 7, 1995

Date of Patent: January 23, 2001

Assignee: UCB, S.A.

Inventors: Changgeng Qian, Tongchuan Li, Tesfaye Biftu, Tsung-Ying Shen

- **Epibatidine and derivatives thereof as cholinergic receptor agonists and antagonists**

Patent number: 6077846

Abstract: This invention relates to the treatment of conditions that can be treated with a nicotinic agonist by administering to a patient an effective amount of a 7-azabicyclo[2.2.1]-heptane or heptene.

Type: Grant

Filed: December 17, 1996

Date of Patent: June 20, 2000

Assignee: UCB, S.A.

Inventors: Changgeng Qian, Tongchuan Li, Tesfaye Biftu, Tsung-Ying Shen

- **Oxadiazole benzenesulfonamides as selective .beta..sub.3 Agonist for the treatment of Diabetes and Obesity**

Patent number: 6034106

Abstract: Oxadiazole substituted benzenesulfonamides are selective .beta..sub.3 adrenergic receptor agonists with very little .beta..sub.1 and .beta..sub.2 adrenergic receptor activity and as such the compounds are capable of increasing lipolysis and energy expenditure in cells. The compounds thus have potent activity in the treatment of Type II diabetes and obesity. The compounds can also be used to lower triglyceride levels and cholesterol levels or raise high density lipoprotein levels or to decrease gut motility. In addition, the compounds can be used to reduced neurogenic inflammation or as antidepressant agents. The compounds are prepared by coupling an aminoalkylphenyl-sulfonamide with an appropriately substituted epoxide. Compositions and methods for the use of the compounds in the treatment of diabetes and obesity and for lowering triglyceride levels and cholesterol levels or raising high density lipoprotein levels or for increasing gut motility are also disclosed.

Type: Grant

Filed: June 4, 1997

Date of Patent: March 7, 2000

Assignee: Merck & Co., Inc.

Inventors: Tesfaye Biftu, Michael H. Fisher, Danqing Dennis Feng, Chan-Hwa Kuo, Gui-Bai Liang, Elizabeth M. Naylor, Ann E. Weber

- **Compounds and methods for the treatment of cardiovascular, inflammatory and immune disorders**

Patent number: 5792776

Abstract: Disubstituted tetrahydrofurans, tetrahydrothiophenes, pyrrolidines and cyclopentanes are disclosed that reduce the chemotaxis and respiratory burst leading to the formation of damaging oxygen radicals of polymorphonuclear leukocytes during an inflammatory or immune response. The compounds exhibit this biological activity by acting as PAF receptor antagonists, by inhibiting the enzyme 5-lipoxygenase, or by exhibiting dual activity, i. e., by acting as both a PAF receptor antagonist and inhibitor of 5-lipoxygenase. A method to treat disorders mediated by PAF and/or leukotrienes is also disclosed, that includes administering an effective amount of one or more of the above-identified compounds or a pharmaceutically acceptable salt thereof, optionally in a pharmaceutically acceptable carrier.

Type: Grant

Filed: June 27, 1994

Date of Patent: August 11, 1998

Assignee: Cytomed, Inc.,

Inventors: Tesfaye Biftu, Ralph Scannell, Xiong Cai, Sajjat Hussoin

- **Compounds and methods for the treatment of cardiovascular, inflammatory and immune disorders**

Patent number: 5780503

Abstract: Disubstituted tetrahydrofurans, tetrahydrothiophenes, pyrrolidines and cyclopentanes are disclosed that reduce the chemotaxis and respiratory burst leading to the formation of damaging oxygen radicals of polymorphonuclear leukocytes during an inflammatory or immune response. The compounds exhibit this biological activity by acting as PAF receptor antagonists, by inhibiting the enzyme 5-lipoxygenase, or by exhibiting dual activity, i. e., by acting as both a PAF receptor antagonist and inhibitor of 5-lipoxygenase. A method to treat disorders mediated by PAF and/or leukotrienes is also disclosed, that includes administering an effective amount of one or more of the above-identified compounds or a pharmaceutically acceptable salt thereof, optionally in a pharmaceutically acceptable carrier.

Type: Grant

Filed: June 7, 1995

Date of Patent: July 14, 1998

Assignee: Cytomed, Inc.

Inventors: Tesfaye Biftu, Ralph Scannell, Xiong Cai, Sajjat Hussoin

- **Compounds and methods for the treatment of cardiovascular inflammatory and immune disorders**

Patent number: 5741809

Abstract: 2,5-Diaryl tetrahydrofurans, 2,5-diaryl tetrahydrothiophenes, 1,3-diaryl cyclopentanes are disclosed that reduce the chemotaxis and respiratory burst leading to the formation of damaging oxygen radicals of polymorphonuclear leukocytes during an inflammatory or immune response. The compounds exhibit this biological activity by acting as PAF receptor antagonists, by inhibiting the enzyme 5-lipoxygenase, or by exhibiting dual activity, i.e., by acting as both a PAF receptor antagonist and inhibitor of 5-lipoxygenase. Also disclosed is a method to treat disorders mediated by PAF and/or leukotrienes that includes administering an effective amount of one or more of the above-identified compounds or a pharmaceutically acceptable salt thereof, optionally in a pharmaceutically acceptable carrier, to a patient in need of such therapy.

Type: Grant

Filed: June 6, 1995

Date of Patent: April 21, 1998

Assignee: Cytomed, Inc.

Inventors: Tesfaye Biftu, Xiong Cai, Sajjat Hussoin, Gurmit Grewal, T. Y. Shen

- **Compounds and methods for the treatment of cardiovascular, inflammatory and immune disorders**

Patent number: 5681966

Abstract: Enantiomerically enriched disubstituted tetrahydrofurans, tetrahydrothiophenes, pyrrolidines and cyclopentanes are disclosed that reduce the chemotaxis and respiratory burst leading to the formation of damaging oxygen radicals of polymorphonuclear leukocytes during an inflammatory or immune response. The compounds exhibit this biological activity by acting as PAF receptor antagonists, by inhibiting the enzyme 5-lipoxygenase, or by exhibiting dual activity, i.e., by acting as both a PAF receptor antagonist and inhibitor of 5-lipoxygenase. It has been determined that 5-lipoxygenase activity, oral availability, and stability in vivo (for example, glucuronidation rate) can vary significantly among the optical isomers of the disclosed compounds.

Type: Grant

Filed: June 7, 1995

Date of Patent: October 28, 1997

Assignee: Cytomed, Inc.

Inventors: Xiong Cai, Gurmit Grewal, Sajjat Hussoin, Aberra Fura, Ralph Scannell, Tesfaye Biftu

- **Cholesterol lowering compounds**

Patent number: 5506262

Abstract: Disclosed herein are compounds of structural formula (I) ##STR1## which are useful as cholesterol lowering agents. These compounds are also useful as inhibitors of squalene synthetase, inhibitors of fungal growth, inhibitors of farnesyl-protein transferase and farnesylation of the oncogene protein Ras. These compounds are also useful in the treatment of cancer.

Type: Grant

Filed: November 10, 1993

Date of Patent: April 9, 1996

Assignee: Merck & Co., Inc.

Inventors: Robert M. Burk, William H. Parsons, John J. Acton, III, Gregory D. Berger, Tesfaye Biftu, Robert L. Bugianesi, Yuan-Ching P. Chiang, Claude Dufresne, Narindar N. Girotra, Robert W. Marquis, Jr., Chan-Hwa Kuo, Sandra P. Plevyak, Mitree M. Ponpipom, Lori L. Whiting, James D. Bergstrom, Conrad Santini

- **Compounds and methods for the treatment of cardiovascular, inflammatory and immune disorders**

Patent number: 5463083

Abstract: 2,5-Diaryl tetrahydrofurans, 2,5-diaryl tetrahydrothiophenes, 1,3-diaryl cyclopentanes are disclosed that reduce the chemotaxis and respiratory burst leading to the formation of damaging oxygen radicals of polymorphonuclear leukocytes during an inflammatory or immune response. The compounds exhibit this biological activity by acting as PAF receptor antagonists, by inhibiting the enzyme 5-lipoxygenase, or by exhibiting dual activity, i,e., by acting as both a PAF receptor antagonist and inhibitor of 5-lipoxygenase. Also disclosed is a method to treat disorders mediated by PAF and/or leukotrienes that includes administering an effective amount of one or more of the above-identified compounds or a pharmaceutically acceptable salt thereof, optionally in a pharmaceutically acceptable carrier, to a patient in need of such therapy.

Type: Grant

Filed: January 6, 1994

Date of Patent: October 31, 1995

Assignee: Cytomed, Inc.

Inventors: Tesfaye Biftu, Xiong Cai, Sajjet Hussion, Gurmit Grewal, T. Y. Shen

- **Cholesterol-lowering agents**

Patent number: 5447717

Abstract: This invention relates to compounds of structural formula (I): ##STR1## which are squalene synthase inhibitors and thus useful as cholesterol lowering agents and antifungal agents. These compounds are also inhibitors of farnesyl protein transferass and farnesylation of the oncogene protein Ras and thus useful in treating cancer.

Type: Grant

Filed: February 25, 1993

Date of Patent: September 5, 1995

Assignee: Merck & Co., Inc.

Inventor: Tesfaye Biftu

- **Cholesterol-lowering agents**

Patent number: 5369125

Abstract: This invention relates to compounds of structural formula (I): ##STR1## which are squalene synthase inhibitors and thus useful as cholesterol lowering agents and antifungal agents. These compounds are also inhibitors of farnesyl protein transferase and farnesylation of the oncogene protein Ras and thus useful in treating cancer.

Type: Grant

Filed: March 19, 1993

Date of Patent: November 29, 1994

Assignee: Merck & Co., Inc.

Inventors: Gregory D. Berger, James D. Bergstrom, Tesfaye Biftu, Robert L. Bugianesi, Robert M. Burk, Narindar N. Girotra, C. H. Kuo, William H. Parsons, Mitree M. Ponpipom, Lori L. Whiting

- **Cholesterol lowering compounds**

Patent number: 5326783

Abstract: This invention is directed to compounds of formula (I) which are novel C3- or C5-acyl sulfonamide, carboxamic acid or tetrazolyl analogs of the Zaragozic acids. These compounds inhibit the enzyme squalene synthase and are useful as cholesterol lowering agents.

Type: Grant

Filed: January 19, 1993

Date of Patent: July 5, 1994

Assignee: Merck & Co., Inc.

Inventors: Tesfaye Biftu, Chan-Hwa Kuo, Conrad Santini

- **1,3-diaryl cyclopentanes and derivatives thereof as PAF antagonists**

Patent number: 5132463

Abstract: Novel 1,3-Diaryl cyclopentanes of the following general formula were prepared. ##STR1## These compounds were found to have potent and specific PAF (Platelet Activating Factor) antagonistic activities and as such useful in the treatment or amelioration of various diseases or disorders mediated by the PAF, for example, hypotension, inflammation, nephritis, stroke and other cardiovascular disorders, asthma, allergic and skin diseases, peptic or stomach ulcer, shock, lung edema, psoriasis, adult respiratory distress syndrome, pain including dental pain, and aggregation of platelets.

Type: Grant

Filed: June 12, 1991

Date of Patent: July 21, 1992

Assignee: Merck & Co., Inc.

Inventors: Donald W. Graham, John C. Chabala, Tesfaye Biftu, Michael N. Chang, Yuan-Ching P. Chiang, Shu S. Yang, Kathryn L. Thompson

- **2,5-diaryl tetrahydrofurans and analogs thereof as PAF antagonists**

Patent number: 5114961

Abstract: The present invention is directed to a specifically substituted tetrahydrofuran of the formula (I) ##STR1## wherein R.sup.4 is an alkylthio, alkylsulfinyl or alkylsulfonyl containing group and at least one of the substituents at positions 3, 4 or 5 contains a heterocyclic, heteroaryl or substituted phenylthio moiety.

Type: Grant

Filed: December 10, 1990

Date of Patent: May 19, 1992

Assignee: Merck & Co., Inc.

Inventors: Tesfaye Biftu, Robert L. Bugianesi, Nirindar N. Girotra, Mitree M. Ponpipom, Soumya P. Sahoo, Chan H. Kuo

- **1,3-diaryl cyclopentanes and derivatives thereof as PAF antagonists**

Patent number: 5047420

Abstract: Novel 1,3-diaryl cyclopentanes of the following general formula were prepared. ##STR1## These compounds were found to have potent and specific PAF (Platelet Activating Factor) antagonistic activities and as such useful in the treatment or amelioration of various diseases or disorders mediate by the PAF, for example, hypotension, inflammation, nephritis, stroke and other cardiovascular disorders, asthma, allergic and skin diseases, peptic or stomach ulcer, shock, lung edema, psoriasis, adult respiratory distress syndrome, pain including dental pain, and aggregation of platelets.

Type: Grant

Filed: August 21, 1989

Date of Patent: September 10, 1991

Assignee: Merck & Co., Inc.

Inventors: Donald W. Graham, Tesfaye Biftu, John C. Chabala, Michael N. Chang, Yuan-Ching P. Chiang, Kathryn L. Thompson, Shu S. Yang

- **2,5-diaryl tetrahydrofurans and analogs thereof as PAF antagonists**

Patent number: 5011847

Abstract: The present invention is directed to a specifically substituted tetrahydrofuran of the formula (I) ##STR1## wherein Ar is a pyridyl, dimethoxy-pyridyl or a dimethoxy-pyrazinyl group, R.sup.4 is an alkylthio, alkylsulfinyl or alkylsulfonyl containing group, Y is an alkyl or substituted alkyl group, R.sup.6 is an alkyl or a substituted alkyl and the substituents at positions 3, 4 and 5 are acyclic.

Type: Grant

Filed: June 8, 1989

Date of Patent: April 30, 1991

Assignee: Merck & Co., Inc.

Inventors: Tesfaye Biftu, Mitree M. Ponpipom, Nirindar N. Girotra

- **Certain 2,5-diaryl tetrahydrofurans and analogs thereof as PAF antagonists**

Patent number: 5010100

Abstract: The present invention is directed to a specifically substituted tetrahydrofuran of the formula (I) ##STR1## wherein $R.sup.4$ is an alkylthio, alkylsulfinyl or alkylsulfonyl containing group, Y is an alkyl or substituted alkyl group and $R.sup.6$ is an alkoxy or a substituted alkoxy or alkyl group.

Type: Grant

Filed: June 8, 1989

Date of Patent: April 23, 1991

Assignee: Merck & Co. Inc.

Inventors: Tesfaye Biftu, John C. Chabala, Robert L. Bugianesi, Mitree M. Ponpipom, Soumya P. Sahoo

- **2,5-diaryl tetrahydrofurans and analogs thereof as PAF antagonists**

Patent number: 5001123

Abstract: The present invention is directed to a specifically substituted tetrahydrofuran of the formula (I) ##STR1## wherein Ar is a pyridyl, a dimethoxy-pyridyl or dimethoxy-pyrazyl group, R.sup.4 is an alkylthio, alkylsulfinyl or alkylsulfonyl containing group and at least one of the substituents at positions 3,4 or 5 contains a heterocyclic, heteroaryl or substituted phenylthio group.

Type: Grant

Filed: June 8, 1989

Date of Patent: March 19, 1991

Assignee: Merck & Co., Inc.

Inventors: Tesfaye Biftu, Nirindar N. Girotra, Robert L. Bugianesi, Mitree M. Ponpipom, Soumya P. Sahoo, Chan H. Kuo

- **2,5-diaryl tetrahydrofurans and analogs thereof as PAF antagonists**

Patent number: 4996203

Abstract: The present invention is directed to a specifically substituted tetrahydrofuran of the formula (I) ##STR1## wherein R.sup.4 is an alkylthio, alkylsulfinyl or alkylsulfonyl containing group and at least one of the substituents at positions 3,4 or 5 contains a heterocyclic, heteroaryl or substituted phenylthio moiety.

Type: Grant

Filed: June 8, 1989

Date of Patent: February 26, 1991

Assignee: Merck & Co., Inc.

Inventors: Tesfaye Biftu, Robert L. Bugianesi, Nirindar N. Girotra, Mitree M. Ponpipom, Soumya P. Sahoo, Chan H. Kuo

- **2,5-diaryl tetrahydrofurans and analogs thereof as PAF antagonists**

Patent number: 4977146

Abstract: The present invention is directed to a specifically substituted tetrahydrofuran of the formula (I) ##STR1## wherein R.sup.4 is an alkylthio, alkylsulfinyl or alkylsulfonyl containing group, Y is an alkyl or substituted alkyl group, R.sup.6 is an alkyl or a substituted alkyl group and the substituents at positions 3, 4 or 5 are a cyclic.

Type: Grant

Filed: April 11, 1990

Date of Patent: December 11, 1990

Assignee: Merck & Co., Inc.

Inventors: Tesfaye Biftu, Mitree M. Ponpipom, Nirindar N. Girotra

- **2,5-diaryl tetrahydrothiophenes and analogs thereof as PAF-antagonists**

Patent number: 4757084

Abstract: Analogs of 2,5-Diaryl tetrahydrothiophenes which were substituted or unsubstituted on 3,4-positions were prepared. These compounds are found to be leukotriene inhibitors and potent and specific PAF (Platelet Activating Factor) antagonists. They are therefore useful in the treatment of various diseases or disorders mediated by the leukotriene and/or PAF, for example, inflammation, cardiovascular disorder, asthma, lung edema, adult respiratory distress syndrome, pain, and aggregation of platelets.

Type: Grant

Filed: September 13, 1985

Date of Patent: July 12, 1988

Assignee: Merck & Co., Inc.

Inventor: Tesfaye Biftu

- **Method of use of 2,5-diaryl tetrahydrofurans and analogs thereof as PAF-antagonists**

Patent number: 4595693

Abstract: Analogs of 2,5-Diaryl tetrahydrofurans which were substituted or unsubstituted at 3,4-positions were prepared. These compounds are found to have potent and specific PAF (Platelet Activating Factor) antagonistic activities and thereby useful in the treatment of various diseases or disorders mediated by the PAF, for example, inflammation, cardiovascular disorder, asthma, lung edema, adult respiratory distress syndrome, pain, and aggregation of platelets.

Type: Grant

Filed: June 4, 1984

Date of Patent: June 17, 1986

Assignee: Merck & Co., Inc.

Inventors: Tesfaye Biftu, Thomas W. Doebber, San-Bao Hwang, Thomas R. Beattie, Tsung-Ying Shen, Robert Stevenson

- **2,5-Diaryl tetrahydrofurans and analogs thereof as PAF-antagonists**

Patent number: 4539332

Abstract: Analogs of 2,5-Diaryl tetrahydrofurans which were substituted or unsubstituted at 3,4-positions were prepared. These compounds are found to have potent and specific PAF (Platelet Activating Factor) antagonistic activities and thereby useful in the treatment of various diseases or disorders mediated by the PAF, for example, inflammation, cardiovascular disorder, asthma, lung edema, adult respiratory distress syndrome, pain, and aggregation of platelets.

Type: Grant

Filed: November 14, 1983

Date of Patent: September 3, 1985

Assignee: Merck & Co., Inc.

Inventors: Tesfaye Biftu, San-Bao Hwang, Thomas W. Doebber, Thomas R. Beattie, Tsung-Ying Shen

- **5-(2,3-Dihydro-1H-pyrrolizin-5-oyl)-2,3-dihydro-1H-pyrrolizine-1-alkanoic or carboxylic acids and use thereof as anti-inflammatory and analgesic agents**

Patent number: 4536512

Abstract: New 5-(2,3-dihydro-1H-pyrrolizin-5-oyl)-, 5-(2,3-dihydro-1H-pyrrolo[2,1-b]thiazol-5-oyl)-, 5-(2,3-dihydro-1H-pyrrolo[2,1-b]imidazol-5-oyl)-, and 5-(2,3-dihydro-1H-pyrrolo[2,1-b]oxazol-5-oyl)-derivatives of substituted 2,3-dihydro-1H-pyrrolizine-1-alkanoic or carboxylic acids have been prepared. They are found to be effective inhibitors of platelet aggregation and are analgesic/anti-inflammatory agents with low ulcerogenic side effects.

Type: Grant

Filed: October 8, 1982

Date of Patent: August 20, 1985

Assignee: Merck & Co., Inc.

Inventors: Tesfaye Biftu, Bruce E. Witzel, Peter L. Barker

- **5-(2,3-Dihydro-1H-pyrrolizin-5-oyl)-2-alkanoic or carboxylic acids and analogs as anti-inflammatory and analgesic agents**

Patent number: 4533671

Abstract: New 5-(2,3-dihydro-1H-pyrrolizin-5-oyl)-, 5-(2,3-dihydro-1H-pyrrolo[2,1-b]thiazol-5-oyl)-, 5-(2,3-dihydro-1H-pyrrolo[2,1-b]imidazol-5-oyl)-, and 5-(2,3-dihydro-1H-pyrrolo[2,1-b]oxazol-5-oyl)-pyrrole-2-alkanoic acid derivatives have been prepared. They are found to be effective inhibitors of platelet aggregation and are analgesic and anti-inflammatory agents with low ulcerogenic side effects.

Type: Grant

Filed: October 8, 1982

Date of Patent: August 6, 1985

Assignee: Merck & Co., Inc.

Inventors: Tesfaye Biftu, Bruce E. Witzel, Peter L. Barker

- **5-(Pyrrol-2-oyl)-1,2-dihydro-3H-pyrrolo [1,2-a]pyrrole derivatives as anti-inflammatory and analgesic agents**

Patent number: 4511724

Abstract: Substituted 5-(pyrrol-2-oyl)1,2-dihydropyrrolo[1,2-a]-pyrrole derivatives have been prepared via decarboxylation of the corresponding 1,7-dicarboxylate prepared from condensation of a dialkyl 1,2-dihydro-3H-pyrrolo[1,2-a]pyrrole-1-7-dicarboxylate-7-carboxylic acid with an appropriately substituted 2-pyrroyl chloride, or conversely, an acid chloride of the former bicyclic compounds with a substituted pyrrole. The compounds are analgesic and anti-inflammatory agents of high activities but low ulcerogenic side effects.

Type: Grant

Filed: December 13, 1982

Date of Patent: April 16, 1985

Assignee: Merck & Co., Inc.

Inventors: Michael N. Chang, Tesfaye Biftu

www.ingramcontent.com/pod-product-compliance
Lightning Source LLC
Chambersburg PA
CBHW070239090526
44586CB00035B/1001